Reflections

ESSAYS ON PLACE AND FAMILY

Reflections

ESSAYS ON PLACE AND FAMILY

by LOUIS J. MASSON

WSU PRESS

Washington State University Press
Pullman, Washington 99164-5910

Washington State University Press
Pullman, Washington 99164-5910

First printing 1996

Many of these essays previously appeared, sometimes in somewhat different form, in *Portland*, the alumni magazine of the University of Portland. "Dollhouses for Daughters" previously appeared in *Left Bank*, and "Between Wars" in *The Critic.*

Library of Congress Cataloging-in-Publication Data

Masson, Louis J., 1942-

Reflections : essays on place and family / Louis J. Masson.

p. cm.

ISBN 0-87422-130-7 (alk. paper).—ISBN 0-87422-131-5 (pbk. : alk. paper)

1. Masson, Louis J., 1942- . 2. Willamette River Valley (Or.)—Biography. 3. College teachers—Oregon—Portland—Biography. 4. Authors, American—20th century—Biography. I. Title.

CT275.M46355A3 1996
979.5'3043'092—dc20
[B] 95-45267
CIP

For Stephanie and Larisa,
Christopher and Caitlin

Contents

Prologue

In the Beginning Was the Word

I CANNOT FIND IN our books of common prayer and liturgies a blessing at the moment of birth for the newborn. Our culture does not stipulate or provide such a ritual greeting; there are no prescribed words. Yet the good news of each life, just as St. John's gospel, begins with words. "In the beginning was the word." Of course none of us remembers the specific words spoken at our birth, words heard through our own crying and struggling to breathe. Nonetheless, we were born into a life of words just as certainly as we were born into a world of air and light.

John's gospel came to mind this summer as I walked from the university library to my office with an armload of books and student essays. Overhead in the unblemished blue, a skywriter began to print the first letter of a word that would float briefly in the heavens like a spindly cloud. The plane was too high and too far away to be seen or heard, and the letters appeared as if by magic or miracle. The letter P was followed by E by P by S by I. I needed no Daniel to interpret the celestial script. A generation proclaimed itself. The word that filled the sky was a marvel of technology rather than a miracle, yet I find in the making of words—even those written in the sky—elements that are spiritual as well as physical.

St. John speaks of the word made flesh, but the reverse is also true. We all attempt to put ourselves and our lives into words. It is a process that distinguishes us and defines us, and is both obvious and mysterious.

Even as I craned my neck to watch the last wispy traces of PEPSI, others watched the ground to catch other writers at their work, and in this case to intervene before letters were formed. Not far from where I stood a teenager sat on a folding metal chair looking over the freshly poured concrete of new sidewalks. He was one of many watchers who were manning their chairs as scarecrows hired to keep vandals from initialing or otherwise defacing the new walkways. I admired the foresight of the administrator who hired the boys, whose reading of human nature was keen: In our culture an unmarked surface seems out of place.

Yet much as I prize order and resent vandalism, I found myself hoping someone would initial at least one square of the concrete. A complete *tabula rasa* countered some cultural need. In the dark of the next night before the concrete finally set, someone scratched some initials and the phrase "Bruce Springsteen lives." And unwittingly the young (I make a presumption here) culprit may have given the singer a measure of immortality. As a lover says in the line of a sonnet, "So long lives this and eyes may see so long lives thee."

Names scratched in concrete become unofficial memorials. When these sidewalks are broken and carted off to some landfill or perhaps covered by some disaster of nature or folly of man, they could become museum pieces. "See," the future will say, "some fellow in the twentieth century scratched these words. Here, touch where he touched." (The scribblings of Greek and Roman schoolboys have remained for you and me to read.) Like books whose marginalia discount their worth in their own time, the initialed sidewalks may appreciate in value if held long enough in the bank of history.

We may attribute the initialed sidewalk to adolescent prankishness, but to do so may overlook our need to express and manifest ourselves, and to give that expression permanence. Even now in Portland's inner city this expression takes a form that is both primeval and threatening. Graffiti that marks the territories of the Bloods and Crips announces the emergence of new tribes among the underclass who have not thrived in the shadows of our sometimes great society. Their proclamations should be taken seriously. These are people who need to be recognized; and to ignore their writings on the walls is to court another wave of vandals in Western society and this time face an enemy from within. The letters on the inner city walls may be our prophecy or our brand of Cain.

As economically and socially displaced as the gangs may seem, their need to stake out their turf, as well as to record themselves and their exploits, mirrors the larger culture. Graffiti has had a place in our history and lore: Daniel Boone, it is said, killed a bear with his hands and immediately carved a record of the event in a tree; "Kilroy was here" was a message left all across North Africa, Europe, and Asia by American troops during the wars. So, too, our need to brand things—usually with a word or letters. Nearly everything we own has a logo. Perhaps God named Adam and Eve, but since then our task has been to name all that we see. And the process of naming has been as important as the names themselves.

At birth we begin to learn sounds. Our name drifts from the gentle noises our families make and becomes tangible, distinct. With the encouragement of our parents the sounds become words and a language. It is a process that defines us, but one that even now we do not really understand. We do not remember a process or mystery or miracle, but rather parents reading to us. With little effort I can see myself, feverish with a cold, wrapped in a blanket and leaning against my mother's side, her finger pointing to a word in a book and her voice reading me stories. After life itself, this is perhaps the greatest gift of mothers. And the so-called "cutting of the apron strings" may not be so much a matter of hormones as it is of mastering language—the mother tongue.

My first day of school (perhaps the first official—and in a very real sense legal—separation from my mother) was also my first formal introduction to grammar and to writing. I can vaguely remember my anxiety at being left in a strange-looking and strange-smelling building. I can also remember my amazement at the letters and words scratched on my desk top. I marveled at the audacity of those children who had preceded me and dared to break taboos. The graffiti in the boy's room held even greater wonders, greater challenges to a decorum that I felt was invulnerable.

Even as we learn to use the tool of language to join and make our way in society, we learn also to use that tool to challenge the society, to test its hold on us, to distinguish in some way our uniqueness. As we grow older we tend to take the mechanics of writing for granted and to regard writing more or less as an intellectual exercise or task. But grammar school is a time of cramped fingers and weary arms. Each of us has had to bend over our letters, to bring hand and eye and mind into concert. I can remember the drills, the lined papers—and in my day, the scratch of the pen and the constant fear of blotting.

The fingers of grammar school children even in this, the age of ball point and felt tip pens, tend to be ink-stained much the way smokers' fingers are colored by nicotine. And the blue or black stains of the ink are perhaps as indicative of addiction as the yellow stains of nicotine. Ink, writing that is, gets into the blood even if we abandon pen and use a word processor.

Most often the letters we practice after we learn the alphabet are the letters of our own name. And how often will we write out that name? We place great value in our signature and take pride in seeing our name in print. Certificates, checks, greeting cards, scrapbooks, the clothing marked for summer camp: all of these are proclamations of our existence and as reassuring as our reflection in a mirror or plate-glass window.

And the reverse is also true. We fear the loss of our names. When our names are replaced by numbers, we question the direction of our society. The tattooed arms of the Holocaust are a reminder of the horrifying dehumanization in our recent past and a warning to avoid the miseries of an Orwellian future. It is no coincidence that Elie Wiesel, who has devoted his life to preserving the memory of the Holocaust, to saving in words those who were numbered for annihilation, and George Orwell, who worried about a future where words might become the property of the state, both prophesied in books. It is almost too easy, in the liberty of our culture and in the wealth of our literature, to take for granted the words and the books that have fostered and guarded that liberty and wealth.

An unspoken or unwritten thought dies with its thinker. A writer gives life to thoughts, and books house and transport thought, mitigating against the old enemies—time and distance—that separate humanity. Mind touches mind but on both sides of the exchange there remains a sense of the flesh as well as the spirit. The very book itself is a physical link between writer and reader. I once saw an interview with the novelist John Updike that was filmed in the room where he writes works admired both critically and popularly. When asked about his sense of accomplishment, Updike took his most recent work, held it fondly in his hand, hefted it almost as if it were a carving, and spoke of it as something made, something crafted, something physically shared. I had a copy of the work on my own study shelves and when I purchased it I held it fondly, and when I had finished reading it, I pondered the man behind the voice. A book invites an intimacy, a kinship, that most often goes unrequited. There are welcome exceptions, however. As an undergraduate very much in the thralls of my first love of poetry I heard readings by the poets Galway Kinnell and Daniel Berrigan. I was too shy (or perhaps too respectful) to ask them to autograph my dog-eared copies of their work. It was enough to stand near the writers who, for very different reasons, touched me. It was enough to be close enough to touch them, to see how otherwise ordinary men could carry extraordinary gifts.

But authors and readers do not escape the crasser trends of a consumer society. A reading or autograph session can become a carnival or media event, though an interesting one where commercial and aesthetic interests seesaw rather congenially. I happened on such an event while browsing among the stacks at Powell's Bookstore in Portland, which proclaims itself the largest bookstore in the world.

Hundreds of Portlanders queued in a line that snaked through the aisles and ended at a table where sat Jimmy Carter. Each customer clutched his or her copy of *An Outdoor Journal* and anticipated a very brief moment with the former president. The crowd was diverse enough to dispel any notion that they were all nostalgic Democrats. A signed book was a piece of history, as in a sense all books are. For those of the crowd who were readers the autograph and the handsome smile bestowed a special poignancy: a sense of the writer as well as his writing.

Whether president or citizen we journey through life with and through words. Though I wasn't in the line at Powell's, it was an image of life: We travel through aisles of words and books. As our life closes, words may very well be our last tie and our final comfort before our mind closes on itself. During my own father's last illness he asked us to read to him, to speak to him even though he could no longer answer. There was nothing unusual in this, for at the end there must be words, too. We come full circle. But at the end there are prayers and liturgies. And for some of us the hope that we will be remembered in words as well as thought; the hope that some mention of us, written or spoken, will carry us beyond the generation where we lived and died.

Part I

Reflections on the Willamette

Reflections on the Willamette

"You want to know
something about rivers,
friends and neighbors?"
—Ken Kesey

When Ishmael begins his story in *Moby Dick*, he speaks about the powerful attraction of water. "There is magic in it," he tells us. Even small pools and streams possess an enchantment that eventually lures Ishmael to his great adventures at sea.

Like Ishmael, I was born in Massachusetts. Unlike him, I grew up inland among the Berkshire Hills. Yet one of my earliest and fondest childhood memories is of a Massachusetts stream. After mass on Sunday mornings, my father and I would cross a bridge on our walk home. I was small enough to lean through the lowest of the wooden guard rails. It was our custom, and my delight, to drop sticks from one side of the bridge and then race to the other to see whose stick emerged first. "Pooh-sticks" we called this game, a pastime we borrowed from Winnie the Pooh and Christopher Robin. Leaning out over that humble branch of the Housatonic River, I had some inkling of the thrill and awe that water could excite. I wondered where the sticks went when they drifted around the first bend and out of our sight, and I wondered where the water came from. Like Ishmael, I was drawn to the water, but I did not follow him to sea. My journey was to the banks of the Willamette River.

During the sixteen years I have lived within walking distance of the Willamette, there have been few days when I have not paused to river-watch. The spell of the water has changed but not diminished. Different expectations yield different rewards. I have not thrown many "Pooh-sticks," but I have pondered by the riverside. Water invites us to reflect. It nurtures the artist and philosopher within us, as well as the explorer. There are adventures to be had on the Willamette, though not the drama of Melville's high seas. For me the Willamette offers quieter, subtler encounters, pleasures requiring slow time and Thoreauvian patience.

Certainly the Willamette rewards the eye; its beauty can be overwhelming. Yet the real magic, the true reward, of river-watching may be more than a bounty of visual delight. For the Willamette River appeals to the soul as well as the senses. There can be no definitive vision of a river. Ultimately, it exceeds one man's life and grasp and there is no end to its reflections.

The Art Brooks Memorial Bench

"To stick your hands into the river
is to feel the cords that bind the
earth together in one piece."
—Barry Holstun Lopez

"Time is the river. We are
the islands."
—Edwin Way Teale

FOR A LONG TIME I've regarded the Art Brooks Memorial Bench as my endowed chair. Perhaps it is a shared endowment, but I've yet to see another claimant. The bench overlooks the Willamette River from a tract of land aptly named The Overlook, an area on the east side of the river in Portland that an enterprising developer platted in the early 1900s. His name is imprinted in several squares of sidewalk by my house: Wemme, 1907. The letters are obscured by moss and chalk lines from hopscotch games, and the script, like the horse rings rusting on the curb stones, speaks of the turn of the century.

The bench, too, has an inscription: *Art Brooks Memorial Bench 1981*. The lettering is simple; carved in the side of the two-by-fours that form the seat, it is the style that one might use to carve initials within a heart on a birch or sycamore trunk. The bench is erected on an odd scrap of land as a memorial to a good neighbor. I did not know Art Brooks, but I saw him watching the river. Norman Rockwell could have used him as a model for one of his characters. He was an original and real. And he watched the river. River-watching, then, is the duty of those who occupy the bench.

I come often to the bench, usually in the evening, often with one of my children and our puppy (the bench comfortably sits one thin adult, one child, and one puppy—if neither the puppy nor the child squirm). The grassy area behind the bench is just large enough for touch football—say three or four on a side. A lone apple tree that in summer bears more children than fruit keeps the bench company. It is a place for contemplation. The river beckons and my eyes always respond. They leap to the river as naturally as children to a puddle. Do we ever outgrow the bewitchment? Siren, sorceress, enchantress—water remains magical and mystical. Easily touched but difficult to hold, she sustains life. Water dictates how we live and where we live. Upon her mysterious surface, we must have first beheld our own image, our first reflection. In pools and puddles, rivers and creeks, we must have first seen our world recreated. Water was our first looking glass, our first gallery of images, and time has not entirely diminished her power or her spell. Here, at the Art Brooks Memorial Bench, I find allure and magic in reflections on the Willamette.

I choose to see this site as mid-river: a present between an immeasurable past and future, a quiet spot between the source and the mouth of Oregon's own river. Of the river's beginning and end I have had experience. Of the past and the future I have evidence and intimations.

A river, like a day or a season, repeats itself. The McKenzie flows into the Willamette; Indian Creek flows into the McKenzie; a streamlet without a name flows into Indian Creek. I choose this streamlet, which can be dammed with one hand, as the source of the Willamette. Here the river was born and baptized in its own waters without ceremony. Other streamlets would do as well, for every creek is fed by countless streamlets and the creeks themselves are countless. Goodman, Hill, Hospital, Burnt Bridge, Rhodes, Leapfrog, Short, Carpet, Fern, Hazel, Chilly, Trout—they spill across a map like the veins on a leaf, like the veins beneath our own skin. Alone how small these trickles seem. But each streamlet rushes ultimately to the sea.

At Kelly Point Park where the fluffy seeds of the cottonwood (my children call them wishes) drift in the air with the tiger swallowtail butterflies, the Willamette joins the Columbia and ends. A line of pilings extends into the confluence of the two rivers like a nearly submerged picket fence. The rivers are neighbors without a quarrel and mingle peacefully. I sat at the point early one summer evening. The sand of the beach bore only my tracks and those of some waffle-footed Friday who had jogged across this stretch earlier in the morning. I never saw him. In the park behind me, children played; I could hear them at their games. And the boys of summer were at their game also; I heard the crack of their bats resounding deeper in the park. But I was alone with the river. A Korean freighter passed by Sauvie Island and moved out into the Columbia. I watched the freighter, *The Ocean Beauty*, and the two great rivers and thousands of cottonwood wishes drift toward the Pacific nearly unobserved and also without ceremony.

All along its course, from beginning to end, the Willamette presents an ever-changing scene. From my bench much of what I see was not there a decade ago: the Fremont Bridge, many of the buildings that scrape high in the sky, Ports of Call with its pagoda roofing, the Coast Guard station. When one of my children river-watches by my side, I can point to where a submarine once was tied at the end of Swan Island Lagoon; where the arch of the Fremont was assembled and from where it was floated up the river on barges before being screwed up to its present height; where a pond settled over Mocks Bottom before monster dredgers spewed it full of river sand, displacing the frogs and mallards and providing a playground for dirt bikers.

Children and newcomers are impressed with my observations, my bench lore, but I am careful around old-timers, those who, perhaps, sat of an evening with Art Brooks, those who smile knowingly at my pretensions to age and experience. One old timer remembers when Greeley Avenue did not skirt along the raft yards as it does now. They all remember the old airport, the shipbuilding, and the testing of landing craft in the river during World War II. One tells of old St. Johns drydocks and a Russian ship that went turtle-up, inauspiciously blocking the docks. My neighbor, a submariner during the war, tells me that friction wears away a ship's hull at the water line. In the fresh water of the Willamette, worn plates had given way and turtle-up went the ship. I will probably steal that story, or others, and tell them without footnote, but that too, I believe, is river-watching. My children will steal my stories of the huge statue *Portlandia* riding up the river triumphantly, a latter-day Cleopatra on her barge accepting cheers on the way to her pedestal in downtown Portland. A child in the future will see my snapshots and try to imagine how I felt that day. Much of the river's life must pass this way, anecdotes without benefit of formal historian or archivist. There must be thousands of stories, but like fish jumping, you won't see them unless you go down to the water and watch.

Late in summer, night is a sneak thief who steals our light almost without our knowing. At night the river surface gathers darkness sooner than the crest of the bluff where I watch from the bench. A tug is pushing two barges northward toward the warehouses on the west bank, which cannot be seen clearly. Its running lights reflected in the water speak of its presence. Its passage reminds me of an analogy once offered by a theologian in a discussion of God's omnipotence and man's free will. "God is like a man watching a train on the track or a boat on the river," he said. "Watching from a high place, he can see where they are, where they have been, and where they will go. Yet he does not interfere." The analogy remains with me, but I tinker with it. For me, man is like a god when he views a river. Yet, though one may feel lordly over the river, one cannot be detached or uninterested. River-watching may make you a pantheist, but never a deist. Details draw you out as you draw them in.

On the opposite bank, the street and house lights in the west hills brighten and imitate the clusters of stars in the sky. By the river, Portland becomes a great constellation. I wonder if a pilot looking down over the city could trace the Willamette? Would it be a swerving path of darkness through the massed points of light?

I wonder: Did Art Brooks have such thoughts? At this moment, how many others join me in my watch? On the opposite bank, on the other set of hills, does someone wonder about me? And when I am gone, will someone else stand where Art stood, where I stand now, and think of the Willamette or of the river of men? Art Brooks was aptly named: In a sense we are all brooks flowing like streamlets into the great river.

When I walk home from the bench reflections remain with me. The side street that leads away from the bench is a dark corridor, walled and roofed by hedges and trees. At uneven intervals three street lights interrupt the comfortable darkness. Puddles remain in the road where water has trickled all day from lawn sprinklers. Catching the light from the lamps, each puddle becomes an irregular pane or dark mirror, so many windows that seem to open on trees and lamps in some underworld. My puppy attacks the puddles, and the angry rippled water relinquishes the recognizable images and wears instead its own darkling mask.

Bridges Over Troubled Water

"But at night if you were on the river,
it was another thing."
—V. S. Naipaul

"The brown current ran swiftly out
of the heart of darkness, bearing us
down to the sea."
—Joseph Conrad

In Old Town in Portland a preacher with dubious credentials asks passersby, "If Jesus Christ were alive today and living in Portland, where would you find Him?" On an alley wall not twenty feet from the preacher, someone has spray-painted the words "Jesus lives," and on a mailbox another prophet has sprayed "Jesus saves." Along the sidewalks, broken wine bottles, some still swaddled in brown paper sacks, betoken a loss of many faiths. Bottle and cross, bum and boutique, BMW and shopping cart: All settle too easily in a pattern so familiar that stark and sometimes grim contrasts disappear. At the west end of the Burnside Bridge, a grocery store whose doors seem perpetually open displays shelves of bottled spirits; across the road there is a mission church, and on its open door a photocopied handbill offers a reward for information leading to the capture and arrest of the murderers of an old woman who lived in the Burnside area. From a window above the chapel a group of manikins, more obscene for their lack of limbs than lack of clothes, stare with unblinking eyes at the procession of ungainly figures who never move with haste and whose gait always appears impeded by obscure sores that nag their bodies or souls. Clothed in our unfashionable discards, the vagrants blend into the rubble that collects in the center of the city, visible only when they presume to extend an open hand from their obscurity and ask, "You gotta quarter, buddy?" Below it all the Willamette River flows; dark shadows from the bridge ride on its surface.

When you step down the east embankment of the river, beside the Burnside Bridge and behind Baloney Joe's, an establishment that serves the street people, you enter an underworld that mirrors the world above but does not duplicate it exactly. Though not entirely strange, life here has different rhythms, different risks. Looking at the city from below a bridge invites a change in perspective that is much more than visual. Seen from here the familiar becomes foreign. You become a visitor.

John Smith is an amiable and practiced guide who has recently left the streets to make his way in a more conventional life. I am a half step behind him; he walks with the efficiency or languor (I cannot decide) that I associate with street people. But he is also tall and his walking stride covers a surprising distance. Our shoes leave nearly perfect prints in the gray-brown earth that is neither sand nor dust. Despite the proximity of the river, nothing grows here. This is tired dirt.

Our walk from Baloney Joe's along the river to an encampment by the Ross Island Bridge has taken on the mood of a pilgrimage, a visit to the shrines or ruins of some earlier people who settled here in simpler yet harsher times. We walk from shrine to ruin to monument, pausing at each just long enough for me to ask a couple of questions. Though it is an August morning, it is cold by the water, and my guide moves with increasing speed the further we get from the city.

Rubble blankets much of the ground: jagged pieces of broken concrete sidewalk piled as high as burial mounds, shopping carts or sections of shopping carts twisted into bizarre shapes, and footwear (shoes, boots, sneakers, thongs, slippers) that are never in pairs. We move over the ground with care that becomes so automatic that our eyes are free to wander. Most surfaces within reach of hand bear inscription and decoration. Foremost among them, a nearly life-sized risen Christ stands in the center of this hobo cathedral and cloister.

In jeans and T-shirt, His hands open and arms lowered by His side, the painted Jesus stares straight ahead. It is hard to tell whether his face expresses welcome or terror. His naked feet and hands bear the scarlet marks of the nails. By these wounds we recognize the risen savior, for without them this could be a study of countless young men who have passed this way. My guide conjectures that the artist was a priest or minister. Apocrypha and fact are not uncomfortable companions in a transient community where a month may separate you from a remote past or simply mark an arbitrary division of time in a routine that seems always the present. Under the bridge what you see now is what you have now. Someone has scrawled a message over the picture in white chalk: "Please love me."

Farther on, someone has drawn Christ on the cross. Above the head crowned with thorns in a nearly gothic script the artist has printed the expected "INRI." And above this in a livelier script: "I'm a hobo lover." And above that a sketchy outline of a naked woman seen from behind. Just as often as Christ and His message appear on the walls and columns, so too this transient Venus, or parts of her, also calls out to the lonely.

Smith takes both for granted and gives his special attention to a pillar close by the river. No artist has sketched here a sacred or profane message, but the pillar is not unmarked. The letters slope in an uneven cursive. But for a word they are quite legible.

Smith 77 Beach House Way OR 97214. This is a historical marker noting the homestead of my guide. Nothing remains of the shack that stood here before a police sweep earlier in the summer. He describes what the police carted off in a dump truck: the frame and roof scavenged from construction sites; the shelves dug in the earth; the hinged door; the floor carpeted with rugs recycled from a dumpster; all the care and attention of a patient man ("Time's the one thing we have a lot of"). All that remains is his view of the river. He points to the clock across the river on the Import Plaza. He always knew what time it was.

When we reach our destination, the camp near the Ross Island Bridge, I see duplicates of Smith's cabin. If anything, their view of the river and their spartan dimensions remind me of Thoreau's cabin. Smith tells of the dreams of the people who live there (to live alone in the mountains); of their freedom (they can hop a train to anywhere in the country or even Canada); and their fears (annihilation in a nuclear holocaust). Smith points to RiverPlace, a residential development on the opposite bank and asks, "How much do you think they pay a month?" Without waiting for me, he answers himself, "They haven't got my freedom."

On a clear summer morning when gulls sit on the river like a flock of contented mallards and when young men sitting on wooden spools play poker in a niche carved from the hillside, this life has the appeal of a higher calling. But the river is not always so calm, and my guide, despite his name, is not so typical. Most of the two to three hundred people who live by the river cannot read; many must sell their blood for money. Despite the tidiness of the campsite and the lack of debris, the dust floor is imprinted everywhere with the *fleur de lis* tracks of rats. Henry David did not have to sleep with one eye open, and it is hard to imagine

Whitman with a Bowie knife in his belt. Men who dream of mountains should not have to live under bridges.

We make one last visit to a memorial that Smith says, "Nobody, even the police, know about." Or care about. The inscription is recent, but only part of it is legible. With chalk as blue as the summer sky, a sure hand printed the date (8 9 85), a man's name (the word "David" remains, the last name is smudged), and "Baby Blue." Near this spot the day after the inscription was made, three people—a young girl and two men—shared a bottle of wine and a hobo campfire. They spilled one cap for their lost brothers and sisters. Then they were joined by another man, a stranger. Within minutes the stranger shot Baby Blue and her companions. One of the trio died; perhaps it was "David." The newspapers didn't give names, only a description of the victim: "The victim's body was found near railroad tracks under the bridge. He had long brown hair and a scruffy beard and was wearing blue jeans, dirty sneakers and a blue denim jacket without a shirt." He could have posed for the portrait of the Hobo Jesus.

Back at Baloney Joe's, Smith and I part. He disappears in the crowd of street people who gather here to share talk and the noonday sun. Across the street I see a piece of weathered plywood that has been wired over the opening to what was once a stairway. I remember now what the remnants of the stairway looked like from below: three suspended steps leading nowhere. People find their way to the river nonetheless. Suicides leap from the bridges. Boaters are swept over falls. On the bank of society, the transients fade from our sight and our responsibility. Yet, for all of this, is the river less beautiful? I remember also a ship emerging from the fog. I saw it years ago on the Willamette. The sun cut through the mist for an instant, and the ship, a four-masted schooner, sailed at me as if upon clouds. It was a Flying Dutchman, a phantom for sure, and the most beautiful sight I have ever seen on the river. Later I learned that it was a training ship from South America, and in its recent past had served as a place of torture and execution. Beauty is not detached. The river joins us to the world and we are not joined by water alone.

From the Wheelhouse of the Western Cougar

"The face of the water, in time, became
a wonderful book."
—Mark Twain

"Its scenery is the more suggestive
to the contemplative voyager, and
this day its water was fuller of
reflections than our pages even."
—Henry David Thoreau

FROM THE WHEELHOUSE of the *Western Cougar*, the Willamette River looks narrow. Like a ranger's firewatch tower, the wheelhouse sits high above the deck on metal stilts and is reached by climbing a series of steep metal stairs. This is a workingman's view of the Willamette.

Despite the nomenclature, the wheelhouse has no wheel. Captain Jim Bennett maneuvers the *Cougar* with two throttles. There are other curiosities for the landlubber: oak paneling and molding, carpets, and in the corner a carpet sweeper.

The *Cougar* was built as a logging boat, for herding and towing log rafts and booms on the river. She has been rebuilt (her wheelhouse raised, her sides widened) to push barges. She is not the pride of the Western Transportation Company fleet. Of the *Comet*, a sister ship, Captain Bennett and Lamar Gardner, his deck hand, speak with admiration; the *Cougar*, however, is to be endured. Though I cannot feel it, Bennett senses more than her usual contrariness this morning and suspects a shorn rudder. He backs her out of the dock into the main channel of the river. She is not fast, but the power of her two giant diesels vibrates through the entire boat. This is the power of *Little Toot*, the tug that could, and riding here is a child's tale come true, like being in the cab of a tractor trailer or the engine of a train. As we pull out into the river, towering above the pleasure boats that cruise even at this early hour, we attract the same attention and respect that trains do. Everyone waves. Bennett is too busy to wave back, so I do.

In a real sense, perhaps there are several Willamettes. Certainly there are several visions of the river. The maritime industry, the sportsmen, the pleasure boaters—each has different expectations. They do not always coincide. What is obvious to one man is a surprise to another. For those who work on the river the immediate and the practical come first.

Earlier in the summer I asked Captain Buck Modrow, president of the Pilots' Association, what his favorite parts of the river are. His answer: "The easiest parts."

In the hierarchy of rivermen, the pilots hold a position of eminence and envy. The captains speak of them as an exclusive fraternity. Only after a long apprenticeship on a river, perhaps after years as a tug captain, does a man qualify for pilot apprenticeship. On the Willamette, the pilot has not only the skill to be captain of a tug, but also a knowledge of the river's currents and moods so that he can dock the ships that load and unload in the port. Modrow grew up on the river. Typically, a pilot's life is spent on one river, and to ask him to compare his river with another is a fruitless question. A Pilot cannot be a fickle man. Modrow is a courtly and articulate voice for rivermen. His vision of the river is practical, but tempered with a sense of tradition acquired from experience—his own and his predecessors'. His advice: "There hasn't been great river writing since Mark Twain, and if you want to begin to know a river, spend some time with men who work on it."

Piloting on the Willamette is not physically dangerous, but dangerous nonetheless because a mistake may represent thousands of dollars. The Willamette is a long harbor and a tricky one—the water level varies, and at low water the docks are high and the pilings tender. A boat has to be eased into a berth. The hands of the pilots and captains rein immense power and tonnage. In the close quarters imposed by the narrow banks of the Willamette, the work demands experience and timing and a deft touch. What takes place on the river parallels the activity of the rail yards and trucking lots that occupy the immediate banks, but the scale on the river itself is considerably larger.

Unlike Pilot Modrow, Captain Bennett is a rather taciturn man whose eyes rarely leave the water. In manner and dress he reminds me more of a farmer than a boat captain. As we move along the river he shares apples grown on his property (he is, in fact, a gentleman farmer as well as an officer and gentleman of the river). He has worked the Great Lakes as well as the Willamette.

Below the Sellwood Bridge the Willamette exhibits a decidedly urban and industrial character. Her drydocks and terminals manifest her maritime lineage. The freighters, tankers, tugs, and barges are the traffic of a major shipping lane.

Upstream, a different character reveals itself. No longer a busy commercial thoroughfare, the river and its banks become suburban and residential. Sometimes she seems an alley of water more than a street. Riding in the wheelhouse here is like driving down a residential street in the cab of a truck. You see over the fences. More often than not you are looking into the back yards and kitchens from where the neighborhood watches you with its real face. Bennett and Gardner eye the banks out of habit, their interest drawn to changes that a visitor would never see. As we pass an oversized white Cape Cod on the west shore, Bennett pulls the horn cord twice. No one is in the yard, no one waves from the picture window which gives us a view of two chairs and an unset table. "I'll bet the old lady died," Bennett says, more to the river than to his deckhand or me. Gardner explains that an old couple lived there. Every morning they would get up from their breakfast and wave to the tug. In warm weather they walked out on their patio. A year ago the old woman must have had a stroke because she was in a wheelchair and didn't raise her arm. Then they didn't see the old woman for several weeks and now the old man is gone. "Must be in a nursing home." One small ritual of river life ends.

At the narrowest point the river is deepest, well over a hundred feet. Through this section Bennett is even more alert, if that is possible. This stretch of river he and Gardner refer to as "The Sisters." "The Sisters, that's where the going is tricky," they say. The river crooks and curves and does not seem much wider than the double barges that Bennett must look over as he steers his course. The banks are rocky and sometimes sheer. And in this especially dry summer, rocks appear that have been in hiding for years. The water, like the skin of an ancient woman, has shrunk so that the bones beneath it protrude. "We call it Sisters," they say, "because of all the nuns that used to be there." And midway through this series of curves we reach Marylhurst. In a not-too-distant past the postulants and novices took their recreation on the promontory that we now pass. I have been told by one who was there how they gathered in their white habits and how they sang. Today, a single lawn chair sits like an idle throne. No one waves to us here.

Most notable in the neighborhood is the old Walton house, a landmark left by Bill Walton of professional basketball fame.

The house that Bill built is a sprawling affair in glass and cedar. Even now, carpenters hammer away at an addition. "The new people must have a lot of kids." Ten years do not age a house the way they do an athlete; age is relative, especially from the perspective of the river. Oblivious, the river flows on in a frame of time that dwarfs one man's or one generation's experience.

We pass the mouth of the Clackamas River. A fisherman is launching his boat, a road crew is installing a culvert. Once a town was born here, but it never grew up. Flooding in 1849 discouraged continued settlement of Clackamas City. At this moment perhaps I am the only person in the world to think about a town swept away and forgotten by the Willamette.

Another fisherman follows in our wake as we approach Oregon City, trolling, I suppose, for fish that we might frighten. Common practice, I am told by Bennett, but a ploy that rarely works. He gives me a bit of fishing advice that I file away: Always fish in front of the boat. His theory is that fish are bothered by the pitch of the turning screws.

On an inclement day such as today there is room for a fisherman and the barges, but it is not always so. At the height of the fish runs, the fishermen span the river in a "hogline," and they have traditionally held their spots with a tenacity and recklessness reminiscent of Oregon's pioneer days. The sheriffs' patrol must open a path for the barges.

And if the river is a thoroughfare and fishway, it is also a great playground. Bennett is continually on the alert for water skiers who dart in front of the barges like children running into a street from behind parked cars. They laugh and wave at the blasts from the *Cougar*'s horns, and Bennett wipes his brow and frowns. "You can't stop a tug and two barges on a dime." In high summer, sails dot the Willamette like lily blossoms on a pond. Yet the craft that the rivermen watch with admiration are the sculls. They glide across the river like a gallery of Thomas Eakins paintings come to life. Man, boat, and water join, and in the moment and the movement they seem to glide from the bounds of time into the realm of timeless beauty.

At the falls we exchange our empty barges for full ones. We are now pushing the equivalent of two warehouses of Spillmate Towels, enough to wipe every counter top in the state. The falls loom in the background, and though they do not rival the Niagaras of the world, they share in their power.

Our return trip downriver has only little adventures. Two fishermen catch fish in front of us (proof enough for me that Bennett's theory is sound). A gang of boys who look as if they have ridden their bikes right out of a modern movie, drop their fishing gear and their jeans to "moon" us (the first time in my life I have been so honored—I wonder if Mark Twain shared the same fate). Bennett radios ahead to have a diver waiting for us to check the rudders.

On the return journey, our perspective is reversed. From any angle the river offers contrasts. Old moorings and tumbling foundations whisper of the past. The brilliant tile roof of the new Spaghetti Factory restaurant and the pastels of Portland speak of new investments. Above McCormick Pier the clock tower at the rail station asks us to "Go By Train." Without its wheel, the *River Queen* floats out her retirement as a restaurant, and across the way the *Global Sun* fills its great belly with wheat for the Orient. And as the menus of the *River Queen* are perused for the day's specialty, hobos move out from under the bridges to forage in dumpsters and trash bins.

At the terminal, Bennett eases the barges toward the pilings where they will be moored for the night. I watch Gardner maneuver the huge gray barges with his long boat hook. A mahout of the riverway, he nudges these behemoths into their berths and secures their ropes. A diver awaits the *Cougar*. He steps off the stern, and the Willamette accepts him with a muffled gulp. Dark water hides him from our view. He surfaces and reports that one rudder has been shorn off and sketches what he has seen below. I leave the deliberations to the crew, the diver, and the mechanics. I have my own deliberations, my own reflections. I am fascinated by the diver (and perhaps a bit envious). So much of the river eludes us, and the diver is a witness to scenes that we will never see.

Above the Falls

"It looks as though someone has cast over the fish a throw net made of sunlight."
—Annie Dillard

"And I lean, almost into the water,
My eye always beyond the surface reflections;
I lean, and love these manifold shapes."
—Theodore Roethke

Gypsy Rose Lee once claimed that the real art of a burlesque queen was concealment and not disclosure. Maybe she grew up by a river like the Willamette. Above the Oregon City Falls as you travel on 99 East, the curves of the river peek out through a feathered screen of roadside willows. So frequent are the river's bends and curves that they present the illusion not of a river but of a rosary of ponds and small lakes strung across the valley.

The surrounding countryside reflects changes of mood as well as scene. Below the falls, suburban, urban, and industrial sites claim the banks; above the falls, the rural and agricultural steadily give way to forest. Just a bit beyond the falls there is a sawmill, a very small enterprise, that mills cedar and perfumes that part of the river with the scent of the past. For me it is like opening the door to a closet where I've stored some of my boyhood.

I met myself one summer on the banks beyond the falls: two boys, Jason and Timon, and a dog, Sam the basset hound. In my youth, I fished the West Housatonic in Massachusetts, and I wore the same uniform—sneakers, jeans, jersey—and carried the same pole and reel and pail. My bucket, however, was considerably smaller (either the fishing has gotten better or boys have greater faith now than in my time). The boys sat on folding lawn chairs and took their fishing and their summer leisurely. During the time I watched them, the bucket did not fill up with bluegills or catfish. Among the teasle and mullein, Sam chased fritillaries and cabbage butterflies, also without success. I left them to their youth and thanked them silently for giving me a glimpse of my own.

Often when I am on this strip of the Willamette, I think of another Massachusetts habitue of waterways, Henry David Thoreau. He anticipated me. "Let me live where I will," he wrote in his essay *Walking.* "On this side is the city, on that the wilderness, and ever I am leaving more and more, and withdrawing into this wilderness. . . . I must walk toward Oregon. . . . There is perhaps one more chance for the race left before it arrives on the bank of the Styx; and that is the Lethe of the Pacific." Thoreau never made it to Oregon or to the Willamette, nor have Jason and Timon fished the Concord or the Merrimack or Walden Pond. But they may have experienced them. The Housatonic was my Walden; the Willamette, perhaps, is theirs. Some locations escape time and place and are charted in the mind and in experience and not on a map.

Miller Ace Mays and Oscar Frederic will give you the best fifty cent ride in Oregon, ferrying you across the Willamette at

Canby and Buena Vista. If you leave your car behind, you might even get to ride back and forth for free. Between them, these two ferry operators have been on the river longer than I have lived. Add all their trips across the Willamette and you have the equivalent of a voyage across the oceans. Repetition does not seem to have dampened the spirits of the operators, perhaps because they deal with the public, for the most part, in the brightest of seasons. The ferries run until the winter high waters threaten to overturn the rafts. One recent summer, Oscar made news by bicycling across the country, no small feat for a man his age. Yet the feat did not surprise me; after limiting his travels for so many years to the width of the river, the thrill of the country's breadth must have been overwhelming.

The road that dips down to this ferry crossing is narrow and winds through farms and fields. At Canby there is a weathered barn in a hay meadow. In front of it, a dozen white beehives sit like tombstones in a country cemetery. Andrew Wyeth could have painted them there. You are more likely to hear tractors than cars along this part of the river. Pickers are busy in the fields.

I share the rail of the ferry *M.J. Lee* with Marvin McGlothlin, a field technician for the Oregon Department of Environmental Quality. Every hour he drops a bucket of sorts into the river and then tests for the oxygen level in the water. I joke that he is doing the blood work for the Willamette's annual physical, and the joke is not far off the mark. The river is in good health. Her beauty is more than surface deep. Ace Mays can remember when it was not so. The reclaiming of the Willamette is an accomplishment too easily forgotten by those of us who do not have his memory of the pollution once so commonplace.

Like a totem, a power pole overlooks the Buena Vista ferry. On the small platform that tops the pole there is an osprey nest.

Oscar Frederic tells me that the birds who built it have not nested there for a couple of seasons, though they are still in the neighborhood. Originally there were powerlines and an even higher pole where ospreys had nested for years. When the line was removed, the smaller pole and platform were a concession to the bird lovers. Apparently the ospreys, after a season on the lower pole, made housing arrangements of their own.

Oscar Frederic shares this sort of river lore the way Ace Miller does good will. The trick to knowing things is study, and the trick to seeing things is to stay still in one place. Oscar's observation post is the deck of the ferry and from it he has seen not only the ospreys but also deer, muskrats, beavers, and, occasionally, buzzards feeding on riverside carrion.

Later in the day I watched six buzzards circling over the fields as I meandered among the back roads on my way to the Wheatland ferry. Many of the fields had already been burned (grass fields I supposed); and those charred blankets of black and brown were intimations of the coming season that otherwise seemed so far away in these fields of summer. Wherever I looked the wealth of the Willamette's water and soil extended to the horizon. As I sped down the highway with my window open, the fields with their different crops passed one after the other like bins in a food market. Some were as fragrant as they were visible. Fields of mint and garlic and onions. Fields also of strawberries and zucchini and corn. Hops, strung over high wires, wound among the acres like great festive garlands. And row after row of walnut and filbert trees extended almost beyond sight, their branches arched, so many side aisles in this verdant cathedral by the river.

Unfinished Symphony

"Much of what is
seems to describe a future song."
—James DePreist

"Onward ever,
Lovely river,
Softly call to the sea."
—Sam Simpson

SUMMERTIME AND THE living does seem easy. Down by the riverside the scene and the season coalesce and time stands still, like a mellow note Porgy might hold. We are a happy crowd of two nations: those who make music and those, like me, who listen. Porgy must have his Bess, and the musician desires his audience as much as that audience desires his music.

James DePreist, the conductor of the Oregon Symphony, raises his baton and we stand together as the strains of the "Star Spangled Banner" float out from the bandstand over the crowd gathered for the last of the summer's "Waterfront Classics." The music drifts over and beyond us to the river whose water we cannot see, whose presence is a great space between ourselves and the buildings on the east bank. On these buildings the glow of the setting sun shimmers; great Midas gilds all that he touches.

Our blankets are spread and our baskets and hampers are open. We nibble our cold chicken and carrot sticks; we sip our Cincinnati Select Beer and white wine. Some of us sway to the

Rumanian Rhapsody. All summer long we have done this. Sometimes together. Sometimes alone, jogging with a Walkman playing to our ear. The music we play at the Willamette's banks are notes in an unfolding composition that reaches out of a past hidden from our vision, hidden as the streamlets that conspire in the Cascades to bring forth a river. If I belonged to that other nation, the music makers, I would dream of recreating the Willamette's music in a symphonic poem. How I'd love to be Oregon's Smetana and transcribe the Willamette as he did the River Moldau as it flowed through and across Bohemia. The land, the history, the legends, the people, the cities—all of these Smetana wove into his symphonic poem. His is an idea worth stealing.

How would I begin? With silence. Like a man, a river begins microscopically. A river is conceived in melting snow and shrouding mists, in the nearly imperceptible and inaudible transformation of gases and solids into liquid, in the showers that patter in the treetops and drip to the ground. Ever-growing and ever-swelling, droplets to drops to rivulets to brook to runlet to streamlet to stream to tributary to river. And downward and seaward flows the Willamette. Her rhythms vary and her notes multiply. She runs, falls, cascades, swells, meanders, billows, ripples, dashes, surges, splashes, swirls, murmurs, gushes, whispers, gurgles, roars; and if you listen closely, she talks and sings.

James DePreist has lowered his baton and is introducing the next piece on the program, "March from the Raiders of the Lost Ark." Overhead, the sky remains day-blue and barely punctuated. One wispy comma from a jet's stream evaporates. One red balloon floats from its mooring and drifts away so quickly that it soon becomes a small black dot in the sky. A flock of starlings squawks a dissonant serenade on its way upstream. A lone heron follows. Humans are not the only ones to bring sound to the river.

The river's symphony would have to include the wild notes, too. Carp and salmon, geese and ducks, beavers and deer: all contribute their unique sounds. Countless shore birds, often unseen, sing a background chorus. Though they play in a minor key, the buzzing and humming insects should have a place in the orchestration. Even now, a dragonfly helicopters over the audience. It searches for loitering mosquitoes and ignores DePreist's interpretation of "Les Preludes."

As the orchestra plays, boats pass by. I see the mast of a sailboat and the wheelhouse roof of a tug. I cannot hear them passing, but I know that they contribute to the Willamette's score. Men have been upon the river for ages and theirs is the sound of history. Those first dusky rivermen can only be imagined. No longer do they dip their cedar paddles into the Willamette; nor does their laughter or wailing ever intrude upon the waters. The strange syllables of their tongue no longer remind us that other nations, other villages, have lived on the banks of this river. But if their villages have disappeared, so too have Multnomah City and Linn City and Lincoln and Wheatland.

At Buena Vista, the ferry hums across the river pulled by electrically powered cables. There is hardly a sound. The idling engines of the waiting cars and trucks are noisier. How different is this from the fording of the pioneers on their way from Independence, Missouri, to Independence, Oregon? How much more noise there must have been then. Did the animals balk at the river's edge? Did the children splash? Did men curse? Did the wagons creak and groan? These too are Willamette music.

What we do know now, and take for granted, is the great din of today's traffic and industry on the Willamette. Diesel-powered tugs and their barges are always before us, as are tankers and cargo ships whose size would be incomprehensible to the first Oregon explorers. The great chorus of humanity that has lived and died by the river must exceed the wildest dream of those settlers and pioneers.

And as James DePreist prepares to conclude his program with "The 1812 Overture," I let his notes be my notes. The night is upon us and the music swells to the overture's triumphant conclusion. In my mind the years roll on with the river, and as I anticipate the percussion of the final movement, I hear the echoes of Independence Days and New Year's Eves, when fireworks and blasts from ships' horns celebrate birth in our natural and national life. Fireworks from a barge in the middle of the river shoot into the sky and burst into exotic blossoms. Sparks fall from the sky, and by the seawall you can hear them sizzle as they hit the water. Finally the echoes that thundered among the downtown buildings cease. The musicians put away their instruments. We go home. But we take with us the river and its symphony, and the music plays on and on.

Evensong

EACH SEASON HAS its own harbingers. When I lived in the East, I marked the coming of spring by the arrival of the first robin in my yard. Soon after, evenings would resound with a chorus of robins singing an impressive overture. When I moved to the Northwest, I found hardier robins who seemed to stay put for the year. I had to look elsewhere for heralds and choruses.

My stay in the Northwest began many years ago, and early on I lived very close to the university in a small Cape Cod on Willamette Boulevard. It was not a quiet place to live. I soon grew accustomed, however, to the sounds from the highway, the railroad, and the shipyards that reached my bedroom window at home and my office window on campus. I even took them for granted. But near the end of my first winter in the neighborhood, a new sound appeared. A night sound was born in the darkness of Mocks Bottom, the isolated low land of willows, dredged sand, and irregular ponds at the base of the bluff that slopes precipitously from the university campus.

The chorus floated on the updrafts from the lowlands like the scent of something sweet. Hardly noticeable, it would hide from me as I passed certain buildings or trees. Amid the din of the traffic, the freight trains, and shipyards, it was an unfamiliar and foreign melody. I had to become a patient and unprejudiced listener before I recognized the rhythm and realized I was listening to tree frogs.

On a balmy night I took a flashlight and climbed down the bluff through a tangle of blackberry vines. Once below the rim, the volume of the frogs' chorus increased. It grew louder still as I moved across the railroad tracks and through the clusters of ponds and shallow pools that filled every low spot among the dunes.

By day, the bottom was not a pretty place. Scraggly willows brought very little color to the dun soil that resisted all but the hardiest weeds. The shallow pools were destined to short lives. The air reeked of industry, railway ties, and dust, even in the wet season. By night, in the glare of the flashlight, the scenery was not better, although it was starker and perhaps a bit frightening and depressing: hardly the place for the pulsating chorus that surrounded and nearly overwhelmed me. Hundreds of tree frogs clung to the willow branches, a tumult of breeding. The frogs' collective voice drowned out the mechanical discord of railroad, highway, and shipyard. Yet the frogs were hard to see, for wherever I shone my light they froze and would have passed for leaves or gnarls if it weren't for the glints reflected by their eyes. I couldn't catch any of them chirping no matter how quickly I turned with my flashlight. So I participated in the orchestration as a guest conductor waving my EVERREADY as a baton, silencing a section here, a section there. Only a person as tone deaf as I could appreciate my glee in leading so large a chorus. It was akin to startling an immense flock of birds into flight with the wave of an arm. Never before had my gestures commanded such immediate response.

I performed with the frogs only on that one balmy night. Had I been twenty years younger I might have returned with a wide-mouthed Mason jar to collect their jelly-covered eggs and wait for the tadpoles to hatch. But I had polliwogs of my own and a busy life on the top of the bluff. I settled for one brief sojourn in the small wildness of that neglected plot of land.

The chorus had been free, so I walked away from the frogs without even ticket stubs in my pocket. What I took from them could be carried with empty hands. The poet priest Gerard Manley Hopkins could say that "My heart in hiding/Stirred for a bird." I didn't feel up to expressing quite the same sentiment for a frog, despite my affection for the muppet Kermit. I did not find them endearing creatures. Theirs was not the music of the spheres; their notes were disturbing and primeval. If there is a cathedral of nature, then the frogs most likely sang the first evensong. Their song foreshadowed all song. In the darkness of Mocks Bottom, the world seemed smaller; in the sound of the frogs, it seemed older. The marvel was that something so primitive and wild persisted.

I left the frogs to their rite of spring, satisfied by the thought that each year I could look forward to their chorus. For five years they did not disappoint me. Yet they were hardly proprietary, and too quickly they surrendered their lease to more commercial interests. Dredgers and bulldozers raised and leveled Mocks Bottom for other occupants. The chorus of the frogs ceased; there was no counterpoint to the dissonance of the city.

I had to travel further into the year and a few miles from Mocks Bottom before I had another encounter like the evening among the frogs. On Sauvie Island I began what has now become a personal tradition of truancy on summer afternoons. When the mood is right and chore list short, I am given to meandering among the meadows and pastures that slope from Sauvie Island Road to the Multnomah Channel. Much as I admire the remote (those places the poet Robert Frost calls "lovely, dark and deep"), I inherited from my mother a New Englander's preference for tamer border sites. I am most comfortable meeting the wild halfway, where the city merges with the country and the farm blends into the forest. I suspect that most of us have met the wild there, probably in our youth, when we or a wild creature crossed the border in a friendly foray. I am especially fond of cowpaths, meadow ponds, and neglected fences that have been enjoined by saplings and enlaced by morning glories. Here the two worlds, the wild and the domestic, converge and sometimes merge.

Along the cowpaths on Sauvie Island the pointed tracks of blacktailed deer were superimposed on the broad, flat trampings of heifers. The farmer's collie, a stray cat, possum, coon, and the farmer himself left a record of their visits around the meadow ponds. In the fields the shrivelled carcass of a spring calf lay in weeds like a discarded leather jacket, and odd tufts of fur remained of rabbits who did not escape the fox or hawk. Life and death knew no borders.

Not all of my meanderings along these borders were diurnal. I stayed once to watch the stars come out. On a windless night I sat in the high grass in the middle of a meadow listening to the last complaints of the heifers and the first movement of the bullfrogs' symphony from the meadow ponds. I had a flashlight to find my way, but I had not switched it on. Despite the stillness of the air, the knee-high grass swished with movement, and a rapping of snorts, whinnies, and neighs quickly encircled me. Blacktailed deer were taking their turn in the meadow. The noise was very much like that of a barn at night. I listened long before I stood and shined my light in the eyes that formed a perfect circle around me. Deer strike me as gentle creatures, but I felt fearful as well as excited by the living fence around me. Perhaps it was the embarrassment of overheard chatter or chants not intended for outsiders. I had broken a small covenant. I switched off the light and found my way as best I could. The circle opened, I left, the deer remained.

I've often wondered what impression I've made on the wild things I've surprised or interrupted, especially those who have looked me in the eye. I remember as a boy kneeling at dusk among brown cattail stalks during an especially late Indian summer. A muskrat, most likely born the previous spring, swam through a channel and stopped within an arm's reach. He seemed to be conversing to himself in muskrat, and he displayed no signs of alarm. Interest perhaps. For my part the eyeballing was one of those endless moments when you hold your breath to freeze time. And then the muskrat with his slicked-back hair went about his business. His first winter awaited him. And I, with my own hair greased back in the ducktailed fashion of the day, ran home to tell my family that I had seen a muskrat and that I was just this far away from him. In my innocence I firmly believed I had equally impressed the muskrat. As he had become part of my mythology, I firmly believed I had become part of his. As a youth I did not think of nature as an analogous or parallel world; it was mysterious and wonderful but not separate. It was an innocence we too soon outgrow. When we become self-conscious we repeat the fate of Adam, and we distance ourselves from the natural as well as the divine. Our ancestors weren't driven from the garden, they simply failed to see what was all around them. Perhaps the wisdom of maturity is a recovery of our youthful vision. Unfortunately we are fettered by our business, and the odds for experiencing the unexpected are diminished. The encounters for most of us are too rare.

In winter this is especially true. One has to search out a different kind of territory for encounters. I find some during the rainy months when I spend less time out of doors and more time at my desk in and among the books where I make my living. I find them in the works of writers who chose to be voices in the wilderness. These are writers who do not belong to a school or an organized group. In some cases the voice of the book has outlived the author. Like all books, at least like books good and great, they first lived in the solitude defined by their particular styles and unique visions. There is a kind of loneliness in single volumes even when they are shelved together in the literary tenements of a professor's office. The true society of books exists in the minds of readers. Yet when the distinctive voices of many writers gather around similar thoughts, like frogs by a spring pool, a chorus grows.

I have in mind those writers who have not lost sight of the wild garden and who continue to bring us reports of what they have seen. I have my favorites: Thoreau, Edwin Way Teale, Loren Eiseley, Annie Dillard, and Barry Lopez. They are writers who tell us that encounters are still possible. They are as likely to explore the commonplace as they are the exotic and remote. It is not what they see but *how* they see that distinguishes their writing. Many of their works are plotted as the unfolding of a day or a season or a year. They keep for the rest of us daybooks and diaries that remain as reflections as well as records. The wild world is shrinking and disappearing and they have chosen to travel to the borders, near and far, and share their findings lest we forget.

I heard one of these writers speak this past winter in an old Portland church. The occasion was secular, a writers' lecture series, but the setting was especially appropriate. The audience I joined could very well have been parishioners gathered for evensong. We listened to Barry Lopez, who like so many nature writers is a bit of a homilist. I believe that nature writers are born savers and preservers whose gift is to put up every season their harvest like so many Mason jars. Yet they would not have us mistake preserves for the real thing. A muskrat on a page is not a muskrat in a pond. The greatest tragedy would be if the wild world of the future existed only or mostly in books or films. In one of his books Lopez observes that "... one of the oldest dreams of mankind is to find a dignity that might include all living things." He shared the same thought with us that night. It was a warning as well. The fate of the wilderness lies finally not with the nature writers but with their readers. The remote—the tundras and rain forest—will not be safe unless we treasure the near, commonplace wild. I was not discouraged by the warning that night because there were so many others there listening as I was. The chorus of nature writers was not unheard.

As this winter ends I am also encouraged by what I see on Mocks Bottom. Over the remaining undeveloped land, the winds and rains of winter have pockmarked the graded sand. Water has begun to stand in shallow pools. Already willow shoots bristle in and around these pools. When the weather warms, I intend to leave my office window open when I work late. And I expect some night, as I sit before my shelves lined with the words of the nature writers, to hear through the open window that other chorus, as the tree frogs again assert their right to spring.

Part II

Seasons

The Miraculous Season

NIGHT, SLEEP, WINTER: The little deaths of days, thoughts, seasons. Against the dimming of their lights glitter stars, dreams, snow. In my memory one follows the other, and every winter begins the same way.

Even now, as I wait for winter in the temperate Northwest, I see the snowbound winters of my New England childhood. Those earliest impressions have become my myths as well as my remembrances. They are a recollection as well as an anticipation of the mystery and miracle of every winter.

I have no sense of a first winter, of a first snowfall. Sometimes looking back is like looking ahead: It is as hard to imagine an end to self-consciousness as it is the beginning of it. The long corridor of memory recedes and dims but does not quite disappear; the seasons and I have always been.

Forever a dark afternoon gives way to a darker evening. There is no moon, there are no stars, there is only the mellow glow of the street lamp that I watch from the window. The first flakes pass between me and the light. I must squint and rub my eyes; my staring strains them. Oddly, it is like trying to spy shooting stars in the summer.

Now the snow comes in clusters, and the light of the street lamp grows softer. I look down the street where the flakes melt like Eucharist on the tongue, slowly, very slowly. The blacktop becomes white; windblown snow gathers like wedding confetti in the gutters. The roads and sidewalks that were so dark are now uniformly white: a photographic negative of the neighborhood. I take that image to bed with me, and I sleep deeply under my covers as snow blankets the world outside.

In the morning the marvel of the world transformed brings the word "miracle" to my careless and spendthrift lips. Only a disaster—flood, fire, volcano, earthquake—could engineer such a change. But snowfalls are rarely disasters, and they can work their magic almost without sound, without disturbing a child's sleep. My childhood delight was to be the first in our house to run out and script the fresh snow with the paths of my footsteps. Snow-covered earth lies before us like a blank page, and it presents conflicting temptations: to leave the unblemished beauty untouched, or to make our marks, record the narrative of our comings and goings. The latent poet always overcomes the contemplative, and step follows step across the white snow. But I hesitated before that first step; in my fiftieth winter I still do. There is an almost unconscious bow of reverence required before a field of snow, as there is (or ought to be) before a blank page.

At day's end, I would peer down from all of the upstairs windows and read back the day. The yard and neighborhood had become pages in a journal. I could trace the duck-footed imprint of my own tracks, and see where my father had set off for work and where he had returned, and notice the path the squirrel took overland from tree to telephone pole, and spy the shortcuts taken by the mailman across the neighbors' lawns and flower beds—liberties unimaginable at any other time of year.

I could also read in the scene the democracy of winter. Even the neighborhood cranks who jealously guarded their property lines through spring, summer, and fall were undone by winter, for the miraculous season ignores or banishes most boundaries. Snow levels and blends, it edits by erasure. And the winter world is deeper and broader than that of the other seasons: Distances look longer, the contours of the land reassert themselves, and trees and buildings recede from prominence.

History and myth agree that we traveled from a garden of summer out toward colder climes. What did the first people do when they saw fields of snow? How did they react when snowflakes showered them? How long, I wonder, before the first snowman was built, the first snowball flung?

Many of our students at the university come from the Pacific islands, paradises of endless summer. For many of them an Oregon winter is their first experience of cold and snow. When snow falls, they are the first to greet it; as they skip classes to play in the cold, their young adulthood and sophistication fall aside, and they frolic like children, tossing handfuls of packed snow. Invariably one of them will stand with eyes closed, arms outstretched, palms upward, tongue extended, waiting as if for a host, for the crystal manna falling from the heavens.

At day's end, tired and chilled after their fun, they leave a journal full of entries on the quad: silent snowmen and snowwomen, the forms of snow-angels molded in the snow, the dots and dashes of exploded snowballs on the trees and brick walls. I read their stories just as I used to read my own marks in the snow.

There is winter in my beard, and my children are nearly grown. It is some time since a snowfall obligated me to pull one of them on a sled through the neighborhood streets. I miss those years; they always brought back my boyhood memories of sliding and skating in the Berkshire Hills of Massachusetts. I did not live near a park then, but there was a hilly pasture nearby, and among children of sliding age the steepest slope was called "Murder Hill." It wasn't much, really. But to a child it was a mountain, just as a pond or lake is an ocean. Growing old robs us of much of that perspective and vision.

I've found, however, that not all of that perspective is taken by age. The city of Portland had one of its rare heavy snowfalls this winter. Though snow never visits Portland for much more than a day or two, the polite Northeasterner in me sought out my almost-unscratched snow shovel and headed out to do the sidewalks. I was a solitary shoveler. I bundled up and pulled my watch cap over my ears so only my nose and gray beard met the winter day directly. I leaned into my shoveling and into the season trying as best I could to clear a broad path that had sharp edges. In a way it was like mowing a lawn, and it struck me how winter reminds me not of fall and spring, which blend into and from it, but of distant summer, its opposite.

In a temperate climate, summer and winter are the extremes: They demand attention, assault the senses, tease and torture with temperature. Perhaps winter is the fairer of the two, since in struggling against it we may warm ourselves. And I grew warm at my shoveling; sore, too, by the time I finished. For a perfectionist, shoveling never ends, for the neat walls and sharp lines of the walks sift or blow away. Mine were unceremoniously scalloped by my old schnauzer, let out of the house, no doubt, to keep me company. Within minutes he too had a beard full of winter.

Dogs are not cursed with a sense of embarrassment, and my helper leapt and rolled and snorted like a puppy until I joined him in play. When he tired, I continued in the careless and frolicsome mood he had initiated. I embraced the occupations of a child in winter. I rolled the first huge lump for a snowman and kept at it, shedding layers of clothing as I warmed in the task. Time fell away with the discarded scarf and coat. I pulled up my watch cap and let winter nip at my ears. Like my dog before me, I let my senses take possession as I hugged and lifted the unevenly rolled cylinders that were to be the midsection and head of my snowman. I felt as if I had rolled the season into a ball, and its coolness was a comfort against my soaked sweater and flushed face.

As the landscape in winter is leveled, so too are sounds. Winter is a time of closed doors and windows. We shut out the neighborhood with the cold and listen to the wind, the mouse in the attic, the creaking of the house's wooden bones. We move inside house and self. True winter humbles us. Within walls and by artificial light, we warm ourselves against the dominion of cold and dark with our musings and our entertainments, our thoughts and stories.

Winter, more than the other seasons, is the one into which we have woven mystery and miracle, myth and magic. For me, Christmas is a season as well as a day, a winter within winter. Christmas Day is but the fifth day of official winter, but in my mind it is the heart of the season and of the entire year. All days lead to and from Christmas, just as in my Catholic culture all roads lead to and from Bethlehem.

Christmases fall over my life like snowfall, blanketing it with memories beyond counting. It is the time for remembrance and linked memories. Each year I bring up from the cellar the boxes marked XMAS. When I was a boy, my family stored similar boxes in a succession of attics. The boxes themselves are old, but everything fits in them just right and replacing them would seem sacrilegious. A box for lights, a box for ornaments, a box for the manger.

My family placed our crèche on sideboards or low tables, eye-level for my brothers and me when we were boys. From the cardboard box we would take out the holy family, the magi, the shepherds, and the animals. Each was wrapped in tissue paper. My brothers and I would arrange the scene, and by some unspoken agreement we duplicated the placings year after year. The crèche I have now I fashioned in the first year of my marriage using wood salvaged from the packing crates of wedding presents. Each year I have to reglue the pieces. My youngest daughter assembles it now on a low chest of drawers, but when she isn't looking, I get on my hands and knees and move the oxen or one of the sheep to where I remember them standing years ago.

I find myself on my knees and staring at the manger at Christmas Eve mass, too. All the better if my family and I have come into the church's light and warmth from the cold of a snowy night. There is much to distract one's thoughts in church: the caroling of the choir, the wafts of after-shave and perfume, the hints of whiskey, the fidgeting of children, the liturgy itself. But I find my eyes coming to rest on the crèche and I hear only the simple gospel story.

How odd, I think, to see a miniature stable housed within the church, and odder still to see a manger within a towering cathedral. Such a simple structure within such a complex one. I suppose the crèche is a sort of temporary altar, just as the manger at home is a seasonal shrine. We do kneel before them, after all. But I am not sure that it is a posture of adoration; like the shepherds and magi and children, we simply want to get a closer look. I believe what we see remains beyond or before doctrinal claims. What we see, more in our hearts than our minds, is Mother and Child, and the ultimate mystery and miracle of every birth, of all love.

That winter birth of so long ago holds such promise that it is hard not to see a world transformed by miracle. And winter conspires with our yearnings and works its own magic. In a landscape where light sparkles, and where snow and shadow make woodblock prints wherever we look, we are receptive to story as well as sensation. As that single stable has become the many churches and cathedrals of the world, so the gospel of that miraculous birth has engendered story after story. Once begotten, a story moves like a winter storm, touching everything in its path;

and so animals speak, Santa comes down the chimney, and the Grinch steals Christmas. I think more stories are told at Christmas than any other time of year. They are our winter births, the imaginary lives we place between ourselves and the cold dark.

After the days of Christmas I am prey to a fleeting melancholy that usually overtakes me the night before I dismantle the tree. Over the years decorating the tree has involved more and more hands, but its taking-down has remained my solitary task. I like to sit alone on that last night when my family has fallen asleep. In the darkened house, I look at the colored bulbs and breathe deeply of the evergreen and let the ghosts of Christmases past revisit one more time. Each year there are more ghosts. Some bear gifts as fragile and beautiful as old glass ornaments. I hold each one carefully and closely, then wrap it and put it away for another year. The next day I fell the tree for the second time. As I drag it off, it leaves in our wake a trail of green and brown needles.

We are not by nature or history true creatures of the indoors, and I think we bring the forest as well as one tree into our winter homes when we return from the back field or the Christmas tree lot. The tale of Bethlehem is not really so old in the succession of winters our kind has known. And the stories we tell, like the years we have lived, are stairs we have climbed through time. Each stair rests on the one below. Before we talked about the mystery and miracle of Bethlehem, we talked to and about the land and found our miracles there. So for me, at least, the tree carries a faint echo of a past almost lost; its death is a bloodless sacrifice not to ancient gods, but to ancient reverences.

Those old reverences are a healthy balm for winter melancholy, so I am pleased to take myself out-of-doors with the proffered tree. The best day for this ritual is one dusted with fresh snow and decorated with icicles, but those are rare days here, and the loss of icicles and the scarlet cardinals of the Northeast is the price I have paid for moving West. But here there are chickadees, who point to the pages that winter has opened before me. They are good guides. To keep their tiny shuttlecock bodies alive they must continually forage among the twigs and branches of the bare trees, where they find seeds and insect eggs too small for me to see. Amid the same branches I see deserted robin and sparrow nests topped with snow like whipped cream in earthen mugs. I see also cones, pods, galls, and if I am lucky, moth cocoons. Life waits in each.

When I was a boy, I collected cocoons and placed them on windowsills. I hatched a part of summer before its time. My luna, cecropia, and polyphemus moths unfolded their velvet wings against a late winter background. I was impatient then, trying to force the next season.

Now I leave the cocoons where I see them. I am no longer in a mood to hasten the seasons. Let the long days of summer come in their own good time. The contours of my life are leveling like a winter landscape, and I begin to wear more and more of winter throughout the year. It feels comfortable. Let the cold come and the snow fall, and in the long nights sleep and dream of what has been and what might be, while the stars glitter above the glittering snow.

Dollhouses for Daughters

MY WOODWORKING TOOLS are a mixed lot. The newest come to me by way of birthdays and Father's Days; the oldest come from garage sales and as part of my patrimony. Like my father, I am an infrequent and journeyman carpenter. But I like the feel of a properly balanced hammer, and the pressure in my palm from a good plane, and the satisfaction of a task completed. What craft my father possessed he passed to me as I handed him the tools that seemed always just beyond his reach. He taught me their names. I do not clearly remember those lessons, nor do I remember naming the tools for my own children. But the passing has been going on for over forty years. There is a difference, however, between my father and myself: His sons held his tools for him, but I have daughters as well as a son.

I did not grow up with sisters and never watched a father grow with his girls. I have wondered at odd moments if my father might have grown to be a different sort of man if one of us had been a girl. And I've wondered if I might have been better prepared for my own fatherhood if I had watched my father with a daughter. There remained some tools, some skills, that I would have to purchase for myself.

For better or for worse, my general fatherly skills are a throwback to my father's approach, or perhaps to the approach of his generation; they are a bit naive and unselfconscious. I suspect the term "parenting" had little currency back then, and even Dr. Spock's bible would have escaped my father. "Gender" and "feminism" and all that these words imply were latent concepts for men like my father. I wish he had lived to see the moments when a daughter has handed me one of his tools. And I wish he could have seen the lives my daughters and I have fashioned together.

Two episodes in particular I store for pleasure and reflection. In both instances my daughters and I built a doll's house. My first daughter asked for a very specific kind of house. From her books *(Mary Poppins* in particular) and from old movies she had mentally designed a three-story Victorian mansion that would cost more than we could afford to spend. On several Saturdays in the weeks before Christmas, she and I found ourselves in a doll house store comparing the finer points of splendidly miniaturized Victorian homes, the fine furnishings of which seemed as costly as real furniture. True to my middle-class roots, I built what I could not afford to buy. A little girl should have the house of her dreams, I thought, and she should have it as a Christmas surprise.

She didn't. Christmas approached more rapidly than my craftsmanship improved, and the secret surprise house became neither a secret nor a surprise. So on the weekends and evenings just before Christmas I had a helper and foreman to hand me tools, to help with the sanding, and to keep my work as close to her dream blueprint as possible. So we measured and planned together. I cannot be certain of her memories but mine hold the remembrance of two people whose perspectives were quite different trying to see through each other's eyes.

I wasn't thinking about varying perspectives at the time, of course. My daughter and I were concerned first and foremost with bent nails, spilt glue, and missing bits of molding that moments before were right there in front of us. But I have since thought a good deal about perspective.

Neither dollhouses nor little girls had any prominence in my childhood; they remained at the edges of my experiences and memories. I have only the vaguest recollections of watching little girls playing with their dollhouses, although I do remember the concentration and seriousness of their play, elements that were foreign to me. I know that all children can focus their attention narrowly when their fantasy world converges with the world we adults call real, and so I expected my daughter's gaze to be directed mostly by her sense of make-believe. But while her imagination did have a lot to do with her vision, I discovered that much more was involved.

We were building a model, I realize now, that was inspired not only by Mary Poppins but also by our family, and by ideal notions of what should go into a home that my daughter had abstracted from her brief but alert nine years. She was figuring not only where the miniature furniture would go but the movements of her miniature family. In her overview she looked through the cutaway back of the house with the eyes of each family member. And her young eyes opened mine.

As the house took shape, both of us would sneak peeks between our working sessions. The cycle of gluing, clamping, and waiting mirrored the frustrations and anticipations of families waiting for real homes to be finished. I felt my skill and ingenuity tested at every turn: the chimney pots, the tricky staircases, the window moldings. But my daughter never doubted our success. Hers was a confidence peculiar, I believe, to daughters, whose special graces include tolerance, amusement, and patience with a father's work. A man couldn't do much better than work with and for a daughter.

If I remember correctly, we were both pleased with our new house. Perhaps we were both surprised. If necessity is the mother of invention, my love fathered a skillfulness beyond my usual talents: It turned out to be a very handsome house. It must have corresponded to my daughter's dream, for she eyed it over and over from every conceivable angle. It measured up. We placed it under the Christmas tree, and it remained there for a week or so. During the holidays I liked to sit in the darkened living room while the rest of the family slept. In the comfortable glow of colored light from the tree, the dollhouse looked real, and I almost regretted the thought of surrendering it to my daughter's room. For it already symbolized something special, and in it I found the telltale touches of its young architect. It was a precocious house of many rooms and staircases, a place of nooks and crannies, a comfortable depository for creative clutter. It was a bold house but slightly old-fashioned. It was, in fact, my daughter.

My daughter took immediate and long possession of her house and kept it in her room long after she was officially too old to indulge in such girlish pastimes. When she left for college, we stored her dollhouse in the cellar, very near the bench where we made it. And when my second daughter was ready for a dollhouse, I proposed that her older sister donate the one in the cellar. But no, the old house was to be saved. So life, as it sometimes will, gave me a second chance to build with a daughter.

My second daughter's house was a very different structure: an airy dwelling of few but large rooms, an uncluttered structure of straight lines. It was a house that she would populate with figurines of mice and rabbits rather than people. (Each of my architects had her own unique vision.) The cycle of sawing, gluing, and clamping was just as pleasurable the second time, and again I could enjoy working with and for my daughter. Hammers and saws we passed back and forth, and some other tools also. It is hard to name all the tools my generous daughters handed me. With love, without judgment, they taught me to bend down and look through windows and doors that I had never looked through before. With them I discovered rooms, walls, and barriers that I hadn't imagined. I suppose I came away from our constructions with a newly calibrated tape measure and a sense that I could measure up to expectations in a new way.

When the house was finished we sanded it, and it too found its way under the Christmas tree, and then into her room. It is still in her room, but it's less used now as she approaches that sad season where we reluctantly put away too much of our childhood. Yet she has exhibited a very literal interest in architecture, and she endlessly sketches designs and floor plans. She may design full-scale buildings someday. That may be her trade.

But my trade is teaching literature, and the only dollhouse I encounter is Henrik Ibsen's century-old play, *A Doll's House*. By choice and coincidence it occupies a place in one of my syllabi every year. In his play Ibsen dramatized the life of a woman who suffered from the misunderstanding and misguided love of the two men who should have cherished and understood her best: her father and her husband. Such suffering is an old story; it is also a contemporary story. Ibsen's heroine, Nora, sees herself as a doll daughter and a doll wife whose life has been confined to a doll's house.

This is a cruel and frightening image of confinement, growing as it does from a child's plaything. Yet the father and husband are not evil men. Their cruelty is not obvious or calculated. They were born and bred blind, and Ibsen's play reveals that blindness. As a dark symbol, Nora's dollhouse is a diagnosis and first step to curing that ingrained and persistent lack of vision. And as I discuss the architecture of the play with my college students, seeing with them its humanity and powerful themes, I watch the young women who know immediately what the play is about and the young men who discover what is at stake. With Nora we all look out from the little windows of comfortable but cruel confinement.

I'm not sure if my students know it, but I try to bring to my teaching the new vision my daughters have taught me. The dollhouses we have built are symbols of that vision, of the perspective I have gained peering through my girls' eyes as we hammered and glued our structures together. They taught me that there are different ways of seeing a doll's house.

I wonder what will become of those two miniatures I've helped build. Will they languish in the corner of our cellar? If my daughters have daughters of their own, will the houses be passed to the next generation? Much as I hate to see these abandoned residences gather dust, I would like my daughters to marry men who would want to build dollhouses for their daughters. Or, quite selfishly, I look forward to getting out my old tools and building dollhouses for them myself.

Of Fathers and Sons

AMONG THE ZEN koans and stories, there is a cautionary tale about a careless man who drops his sword from a moving ship. Before he seeks help, the anguished samurai marks a line on the side of the ship where the sword fell. In the context of the story, he is foolish and suffers the ridicule of the captain and crew who find his line a meaningless mark that bears no true relation to the actual spot where the sword disappeared into the water. I've never approached that tale with quite the right frame of mind, for I've always felt a peculiar sympathy for the man and an admiration for his line, and for his naive attempt to mark a loss.

When I lost my father, I began to scratch some lines of my own. Like other sons, I, too, would "rage, rage against the dying of the light." There was some folly in the gesture, but I was not quite as foolish as the unfortunate samurai who sought to recover his loss. At first I found comfort simply in recording it. Death appeared to stop time, and grief followed the illusion of equilibrium. For once I could look at the life I shared with my father: I could hold it before me and turn it about and come to know what it meant to be both a father and a son. This knowledge I would apportion as part of my patrimony.

Only in childhood does the relationship between father and son seem simple, and then only in the mind of the child. I know this now for I have become a father myself. I have a son named after me just as I was named after my father and he after his father. The names alone do not matter. More than names and genes bind the generations together. Other threads tie us to a shared history and destiny. I remain a link in an unbroken series of promises and expectations. I feel for my father's lineaments on my brow and search for them in my son. I fear my father's weaknesses and pray that my own will not haunt my son. There are ghosts before us, and we may be the ghosts of later generations. (Kindly spirits, I hope.)

Since my father's death I have had a sense of being midpoint between these generations. I am reminded of an optical illusion I experienced as a boy waiting in the ornate and mirrored lobby of a Fox theater. Walking between the mirrors, I could see on either side of me endless lines of my reflected self receding gradually beyond the focus of my eyes. I imagine those columns now as the fathers that preceded me and the sons that will succeed me.

My family gathered the night before we buried my father. There were so few of us that we could sit together in my mother's living room. The last of my father's generation—an older sister and a younger brother, both in their seventies—gave me two stories that allowed me a deeper look in the mirror of the past. My father was an artist, and my aunt remembered when, as a young boy in Atlantic City, he would draw on the boardwalk with charcoal or pastel crayons. Tourists in linen and seersucker applauded and threw coins. These he brought home to his mother as signs of his talent: See, I am an artist. But my grandmother, who brought with her from Ireland a resolute faith, had already promised her God that my father would be a priest. She recoiled from the small chalk-stained hand filled with coins.

Over a stiff whiskey, my uncle told a different story, one that included my grandfather. It was my uncle's belief that his father came to America from France, but not directly. He came instead by way of South America, as an escapee, according to family legend, from a penal colony where he had been sent for political misdeeds. We could accept with more certainty that he had soldiered in Indochina, spoke several languages, and took life as it came. He must have had a very different notion of heaven and earth than my Irish grandmother. His Catholicism was decidedly too catholic for their marriage to last. When my father studied at the seminary, his parents began to live apart. My uncle believed that grandfather earned his living making bootleg gin. In my uncle's story, my father came home to visit his parents, his mother first. She made her young seminarian swear by the Virgin Mother and Holy Mother the Church that when he visited my grandfather he would not take alcohol. My father proudly took the oath. And as promised, my father refused the drink my grandfather offered. He repeated his sacred oath, much, I suspect, to grandfather's amusement. My father did, however, accept diced fruit served in a syrup concocted specially for the occasion; grandfather had the Frenchman's gift for preparing food. His syrup was mostly cognac, and my father, in his innocence, asked for seconds and thirds. He went home drunk, a disgrace to all his holy mothers.

The hand that sketched on the boardwalk guided my own small hand. I remember sitting on my father's lap while he held a drawing pad before us. We took turns scribbling odd lines on the sheets. Then, in turns, we would attempt to modify the lines into some recognizable shape: a tree, a stick man, a sailboat, Mickey Mouse. Invariably my modifications were failures, jumbled lines that would not conform to the picture I had in my mind, scribblings that brought tears to my eyes. And my father then would take my hand in his own so that I was cradled in his arms. Our hands and arms moved as one, and I could feel the movement of his chest as he breathed over our drawing. Together we added a line here, a curve there, and a shape emerged from my squiggles.

The hand that had been promised to the priesthood, that swore a sacred oath: I can see that hand, too. Once in my typically rebellious adolescence, I climbed a nearly sheer face of a gravel quarry. We were on a family outing, and through my impetuosity I sought to challenge my father and earn his pride. My climb ended when loose gravel gave way under my feet before I reached the top. I was stranded and my father had to drive to the nearest farm house for help. An old farmer hoisted me over the top with a length of twine. He hauled up my miserable and rather uneventful life like a bale of hay. On the way I bargained and pleaded with God to spare me. I was saved, of course. When I reached the bottom of the quarry where a small crowd and a state trooper waited with my father and younger brothers, my father, tears streaming over his cheeks, slapped my face. To ease the strain, the old farmer remarked to no one in particular, "Shoot, I must pull two or three kids over the top every summer." To himself my father muttered something about having prayed that I would someday be a priest and now I had nearly killed myself. Much later in life I came across a ritual prayer in one of the novels by the Nigerian, Achebe. His character prays: "May children put their fathers into the earth and not the fathers their children." I understand the tears now and the slap, too. And I realize that many of the skirmishes that troubled our love began long before my birth. Every father is visited by ghosts his son cannot see.

I've held my own children on my lap and guided their hands over a sheet of paper. And like so many others, I've felt the strange sensation of being both father and child. The essayist and author of *Charlotte's Web*, E.B. White, presents a classic description of the experience in "Once More to the Lake." Reliving with his son a summer's vacation that he once shared with his father, White reflects: "I began to sustain the illusion that he was I, and therefore, by simple transportation, that I was my father." There is in White's account a polite, restrained, and nearly impersonal exchange of roles. He speaks ultimately of change and death. Yet my own experiences have rarely been so impersonal or abstract. Quite the opposite. In those moments when I've felt the mingling of the three generations, the eerie slide into the life of my father or son, I've experienced mixed emotions, some pleasurable, others very painful. Invariably I regret that I became a father before I truly realized what it meant to be a son.

My father did not go gentle into that good night. His hospice was in the back wing of a sprawling, one-story hospital. Often in the halls of the hospital, I encountered an old man dressed in a hospital gown literally inching his way down the hallways with the assistance of a wheeled walker. An IV suspended from a pole seemed to fuel his dogged movement. His face bore the anonymity of old age. His journey never varied. Each day he traveled to the maternity ward and stood for several moments staring through the window where the newborns lay in their carefully labelled clear plastic baskets. I never questioned him. There was a gracefulness in his routine that forbade questions. I accepted him as a parable, a preface to my father's ritual. The mystery of life and death were there for anyone willing to see. They were at my father's bed also, and though we talked much, much was left unsaid. My father, who the Irish would have called a "failed priest" and the French a failed artist, settled for a sustaining faith and a small talent. He thanked God for his sons and saw his life as something given rather than something done. I did not argue with him. Nor did I ask the questions I might have asked. During those last long days and nights, my father told me that inside he often felt young, as if he had never grown old. In the delirium and morphia dreams, the man in the bed who was my father thought of himself as a son. At the last we exchanged places.

Since then I think often about the foolish samurai who did not reckon the movement of the boat, and of the hall of mirrors in the movie theater that symbolized the past and the future. And

I remember the last words of White's essay: ". . . suddenly my groin felt the chill of death." Seeing his youth repeated in his son, White sensed his own mortality. Such thoughts occurred to me at my father's bedside; I was chilled and I marked the occasion. Yet I did not ignore my passage in time. I've learned to see the other set of mirrors, the future, where I am reflected in my son.

There is a temptation to accept the future as compensation for the lost past, a son as compensation for a lost father. But time does not allow such desperate and fixed judgements. It is more generous. Instead time blends and blurs; we rarely live in an isolated present. In the lives of our children we relive our own experiences. A child gives us second sight, activates our memory. And as I follow the adventure of my son's life, watching him as a father, I have some notion of what my father felt. Epiphanies occur, but I know enough not to seek them. Glimpses of the past surprise me; I welcome them. The Zen poets have long understood this. I've envied the poet Tairo this haiku:

My good father raged
When I snapped the peony . . .
Precious Memory!

Shared lives persist. Even as I remember, I am becoming a memory for my own son. At the balance point, the past touches us but does not hold us, and we touch the future but should not hold it. Yet I am no mystic; I persist in scratching lines towards an understanding of what it means to be a son and a father. Those lines remain somewhat disconnected, a linear koan. They lie before me like my childish scribblings on the page of my father's drawing pad. I look again and again for the hidden shape and sometimes I feel the pressure of another hand guiding me slowly to its discovery.

Of Windows and Wider Worlds

SEE THE PICTURE through my eyes. Under a crescent moon an elfin figure pipes melody into night winds. His legs are bare. The lines are simple: White etched from a black background. I just saw this picture recently, but the *act* of seeing is printed in my past; as far back as I can remember, pictures like it in books and on walls opened before me like windows to parallel worlds.

Such windows usually catch me unaware, in idle moments. I sit in visitors' chairs, waiting in cluttered offices. Time and courtesy hold me prisoner. So often in life we sit and wait, or sit and endure waiting: gentle confinement, but the mind rebels. My eyes move where my body can't, probe for an opening, seek an escape. That is how I found this wind-blown elf: Tacked to a friend's wall, the picture became a window just large enough for me to squeeze through, and I fled into it for a moment.

This kind of daydreaming is an activity much maligned and undervalued. There are all sorts of daydreams and flights of fancy. Some are rather simplistic, like the fleshing-out of wishes; others are visionary, complex, imaginative journeys. And there are visions and journeys in picture-gazing.

Where did this start, this stepping into pictures? I like to think it began when we first scanned our world from behind the rails of our cribs, or from the shoulders of pacing parents who patted us on the back and made sounds that were music before they were language. Wakened eyes travel relentlessly, and the mind must follow as best it can. For most of us the walls between the windows wore pictures, and to new eyes what is the difference between an open window and framed picture? Did we reach to pull something from the canvas or print, as I have seen my own children do? Do we still reach?

Illustrations have a long history. Perhaps they preceded words; long before we were children, our earliest parents left picture-stories on cave walls. But these are the speculations of adulthood, of reasoned reflection. In childhood I do not remember making such distinctions. Books with pictures were decipherable before I gained mastery over words and phrases. A bedtime story was most often to be seen *and* heard, and the world-read-from and the world-read-about could and did merge.

I remember one such merger of worlds. I must have been very young when it happened, because I remember looking up to my mother—and she is a very small woman. We were in church, where everything towered above me. Walls of winter coats cut off my view of the altar, so I rested my chin on the rounded pew and listened to the choir and to a scratching and thumping sound on the sky-high roof above. I tugged at my mother's sleeve, and midway through the sermon she finally bent her ear to me.

"What is that noise?" I whispered.

"Steeplejacks," whispered my mother.

My best guess now is that branches of the elms that grew by the church were brushing the roof slates. But this was no answer that I'd accept, and my mother knew it. Into my mind flashed steeplejacks, mysterious figures seen only in my bedtime storybook but more real to me then than any elm trees. I saw steeplejacks bobbing their bottoms to the heavens as they plied their trade along the spine of the slanted slate roof and blue-green copper of the church's spire.

Those mergers of picture-worlds and real world came often for me. My family often gathered in the living room on Sunday afternoons, and my two brothers and I would sit uncomfortably on the couch while the adult talk floated over our heads. I would gaze from picture to picture, taking refuge where I could. I took refuge most often in a Grant Wood print called "Spring in Town," which featured a man turning over the soil in his garden. In the distance smaller figures were at work: A woman hanging her wash, a man mowing his lawn, two men beating a rug, a man climbing a ladder to repair a roof. Behind these figures the steeple of a church rose above the houses and trees of the neighborhood.

Had the blinds of the picture window in our living room not been drawn, I might have looked out across the street and watched our neighbor Mr. Archambeaux performing one of those tasks. And had I been sitting in the arm chair, I might have seen not only Mr. Archambeaux but also the spire of St. Mark's and the elms that shared the sky with it. To me all views were real, both painted and not painted. I did not doubt then that the painted world extended beyond the limits imposed by the wooden frame.

My father was an artist, and in our house he hung his originals, some copies of old masters, and an assortment of prints that he rotated with the seasons. I didn't question the presence of pictures any more than I did windows and doors: They were a given in my world. Nor did I think much about who painted or drew which picture. In time I learned to distinguish my father's works from the others, and in time I learned the names of the other artists. But for the most part I had no sense of a creator, or of the pictures as something made. The hand of the artist was as invisible to me as the hand of God.

My mother has moved many times since my youth, and many more times since my father's death, but she still hangs those pictures. Home remains where she lives and where the old pictures hang. To her, as to me, they are more than furnishings; they are portable windows with views both static and alive. Those old paintings are more than decorative markers or touchstones to the past, more than sentimental or nostalgic keepsakes. For pictures are like windows: No matter how humble the view, they offer possibility, challenge, risk. Every invitation to see allows us to add to our creation and interpretation of the world.

And pictures are enlightening, in all senses of the word. I remember that my artist father would often explain matters by pulling a pencil stub from his pocket and sketching on whatever paper came to hand. A doctor who treated me for many years possessed the same gift. He too would reach for paper (usually a piece ripped from the roll used to cover the examining table) and trace the odd goings-on of my insides. Both men used pictures to enlighten, to let in light, to illuminate.

I look again at the picture of the piping fellow in the wind. If I shut my eyes I can hear the elfin melody under the crescent moon. If his song has words they are the lessons of pictures. Look closely. Enjoy. And take care, for to enter a picture is to hazard immersion as well as escape.

The Season of Promise

I HAVE NOW BURIED both of my parents in autumns, and that poignant season casts long and cold shadows into this winter where I wait, more than ever, for the promise of spring. I watch the eastern sky for rainbows and comfort myself by repeating God's pledge to Noah: "I do set my bow in the cloud, and it shall be a token of a covenant between me and the earth." In spring it is easy to believe in that covenant, and that we are all chosen people.

The world is a garden then: Showers wash away the remnants of winter and flood memory with fond old images that blossom perennially. My first remembered spring warms a small, white, frame house that sits on a New England hill. Through its back door I follow my mother into the sunshine. Her dark hair is pulled back in a braided bun. I am too young to know how young she is. My feet slide inside my hand-me-down rubber boots; the boots slide in the ooze beneath black puddles. I stamp the puddles, sharding the reflected sun over and over.

Mother rakes leaves from a rock garden and pulls, by hand, crisp brown swords of last year's irises. I clasp a handful like palms and shuffle through her neat piles of debris. Already this year's plants push through the soil toward summer. From the warmth of one of the rocks a garden snake ribbons through the green shoots toward my booted feet. With the same calm deliberation that she used to clean out the garden bed, my mother deflects the snake back to the rocks with the prongs of the rake.

It is an emblematic moment, but I am too young to see or feel beyond the immediate. Mother, pale shoots, snake: These I register and remember, as well as my feelings—love, awe, an intimation of fear. Childhood is the Eden of every life, and spring the Eden of every year. Childhood we must outlive, but we may relive each spring. The child, the young mother, the garden on a New England hill: They are no more. Yet spring returns, as it always does, to nourish the shoots of memory, to surprise and awe us.

In time I walked out to greet and inspect spring by myself. We had moved from the white house on the hill to a larger house. Like so many other houses in small New England towns, it straddled the line between city and country, and I could walk as easily to farm and woods as I could to store or school. Each year I would take to the meadows and woods in an annual and solitary sojourn to meet spring. I did so in high rubber boots. As I tromped through puddles and wet meadows, the lingering winter cold that began to numb my toes belied the warmth that the unseasonal sun bestowed on my capped head. I was caught between heat and cold, like spring itself.

My search lacked method but it had direction. I would head to the meadow, the woods, the farmers' lots. As I grew, the length of my walks grew apace. The grass in the meadow, free of winter's snow, still told tales of winter. The old leaves were brown and humpbacked from the drifts they had supported. All lay level and matted as a deep rug. Yet the pattern was broken like fabric ravaged by moths: Tunnels and runs of field mice crisscrossed the meadow, and nest-like hollows were evident where cottontail rabbits had slept hidden from the wind. The ghastly pallor of the drifts had been illusory; life had gone on under winter's spell.

Melted snow pooled in small ponds that would disappear before summer. Their water, cold and clear, seemed hard as glass, and the ponds themselves became shallow display cases for last year's leaves. Many leaves had rotted so that only the ribs and veins remained, but these were so complete that they resembled the intricacies of finely netted lace rather than leafy skeletons. In the retreating dampness of these ponds skunk cabbages had already pushed up their mottled spades, which looked like hooded monks lost in prayer. If spring is the morning of the year, it seems appropriate that these plain and mendicant blooms should announce its arrival.

Further into the woods and the season, trillium and jack-in-the-pulpits present themselves. The Trinitarian structure of the trillium and the almost ecclesiastical architecture of the jack-in-the-pulpit allow these flowers, like the skunk cabbage, to announce spring humbly. In the temperate zones, at least, the plant world appears reluctant to offend just-departed winter with a gaudy or vulgar display.

Where the woods adjoined the neighboring farms, signs of spring intertwined in more complicated and disturbing patterns. Spring promises life, but more than flowers emerge from the newly warmed earth. I walked late one spring through trees that ran parallel to a farm road. On either side were shallow gutters of fieldstones, gathered most likely by the first farmers in the area before they could till their soil. The gutters and the leaves at my feet were dry. My feet crunched and swished as I walked over the ground. Overhead the trees were in their first green. When I paused to look up at the new leaves, the swishing and hissing through the leaves at my feet continued, and I noticed that the gutter was undulating. Droves of garter snakes had hibernated in holes beneath the stones; like me, they had been drawn out by the warmth of spring. The boy I was did not have the disinterested eye of a scientist, and the teeming and tangled life squirming about my feet filled me with panic. I wanted to run but was afraid, lest I be snared in an entanglement of snakes. I tiptoed through them, and I never crossed that space again. Even now those serpents squirm from under their rocks into my infrequent nightmares.

There was no danger, no harm, in the garter snakes, but the sight of them had touched a primal chord in me—a chord that would be touched again by other sights as I went on along my many roads.

I remember a glade in the woods where the grass grew greener than the meadows. It was a quiet spot made eerie by the shadows of the trees that surrounded the green. I did not feel welcome there and waited many springs before violating its seclusion and silence. Grass grew strangely from among the carpet of leaves. Amid the grass lay the scattered bones and skulls of long-dead horses. I took one skull home and hung it on a rusty spike in our garage. I suppose it was a trophy of a youthful quest, my passage like a knight of old through the Chapel Perilous.

Deeper still in the same woods stood a chimney of fieldstones. It resembled a stump or an eccentric outcrop of rock rather than a thing of hands, the hearth of a home. Trees pressed in on all sides; leaves and moss carpeted the floor. One short span of wall jutted from the leaves and here and there lay scraps of rusted iron. Barrel rings, broken axles, the head of mattock: It was hard to tell. I left them untouched. Life and death, like the seasons, dance in circles. Here they held hands and the dance was close. It was enough to observe their presence, and move on.

I did not have to journey far to find spring, for we had lilacs in our backyard. When their cluster of white and purple flowers bloomed, the perfume reached us through our open windows and screened back door. Everyone, it seemed, had lilacs in their backyards, and lilacs were a favorite blossom for the altars and shrines of my Catholic childhood. They remain for me a flower of community and faith, in no way diminished by their abundance.

Lilies rather than lilacs adorned the Easter altar, but my favorite spring holy day was later and, to my mind, more seasonable. We brought our lilacs then, great armfuls, to Mary's altars and shrines. And on May day a young girl often crowned a statue of Mary-the-mother-to-be with flowers. The likenesses of Mary that I remember present her as a young woman with dark hair standing barefooted among blossoms; under one of her feet was a serpent. The simplicity of the young woman who would give life was the perfect counterpoint for me to the death and mysteries of Good Friday and the Easter resurrection. Lilacs succeeded lilies; the majesty of the Easter liturgy was succeeded by our song of "Ave, Ave, Ave Maria."

It is in the nature of things for one cycle to hasten to the next. A freak thaw teases flowering trees into premature blossom. Crocuses penetrate the snow in their haste to unfold their flowers. Despite the presence in most flowers of stamens and ovaries, it is tempting to think of flowers in bloom as feminine. Even more so, perhaps, as they lose their petals and swell with seeds that must burst forth before autumn. But it is just as easy to think of the shoots penetrating up through the soil and the snow as masculine. The cellular heat of the thrusting skunk cabbage actually melts the snow it penetrates. The beauty of flowers does not preclude their abandon and insatiable drive to live, to reproduce, to dance in the breeze.

In its haste to begin, life is often vulnerable, at risk. And the natural world is spendthrift and unsentimental. I watched its carelessness during a March thaw on one of the very first days of spring. By rights it should have been a day of snow and ice, but the weather honored the vernal equinox with unseasonable warmth. I had spent the evening dancing with the young woman who would soon be my wife. As we drove home, flushed with youth and the exertion of our dance, we left the windows of my old Dodge open to the breeze. My future wife's home lay in countryside that was once a sandy lowland, marshy and fertile, but had become a hodgepodge of vegetable farms and ranch houses. Earlier that day young men in white tee shirts had waxed and polished their cars; their cans of Simonex still lay atop mounds of snow left over from a recent storm.

These lowlands were also home and breeding ground to toads, which thrived in the easily burrowed soil and in the still waters of countless shallow ditches. Warmth drew them from their hibernation, and we could hear the trilling males through the opened windows of my battered Dodge. The blacktop road that still held the day's heat became a toad road on which they hopped, in most ungainly fashion, to and from the circles of light thrown from utility-pole lamps. Beneath each artificial moon were dozens of toads, each spellbound by the light and oblivious to the infrequent but fatal night traffic.

I slalomed an erratic course, avoiding the toads as best I could. Later, on my way home, I retraced in reverse my journey up Toad Road. But now the cold had set in, and I drove with the windows shut, humming along to a country western station that retired the day with mournful ballads. No toads hopped in my high beams, but their small flattened carcasses spread across the blacktop like lost and empty change purses. Mistaking a day for a season had cost them their lives.

In spring, and in the spring of our lives, we are not immune to the imperatives of life or its risks. I waited one April for the birth of my first child, a dark-haired girl. It was a hard and long delivery but it was also the ultimate promise of life: New life. Each birth is a wonder, and the joy and fear attendant to each are made sharper by the universality of the experience. I waited, I hoped, I prayed, but I did not feel a sense of attachment. I was but witness: One who must wait.

The hospital was a small one that perched on a high bluff overlooking the Willamette River, near Oregon City. Between messages from the delivery room, I looked down on the river. By day it was brown with silt. At night it was black, a dark waving line in the dark night. There were lights in that darkness where fishermen had set salmon lines. Beneath their boats the spring runs of salmon worked upstream against the current to spawn and to die. The salmon had done this for eons beyond imagining; for millennia they had fulfilled the promise of spring and brought forth new life. So it is in the world. When I first held my daughter, I was no longer witness, no longer outsider; she made me part of the circle of life, the circle of human seasons that also dances through time beyond imagining.

I have several children now, and a house, and a garden. It so happens that a lilac blooms by the steps of my back door. I have not lost the urge to greet spring, but with a garden of my own I find I do not travel much beyond my yard. I live in the city, though there is a ravine between highways only a few blocks from my house. Because the ravine is unsuitable for building it has been left to itself. Trillium blossom there, and I make a short pilgrimage each year when I sense their time for blooming.

I travel less and look closer these days. I catch my first sign of the season when mosquitoes dance in a shaft of March sunlight, moving up and down like miniature yo-yos on invisible strings. When the winter rains cease, I take rake and spade to my garden. For years I also took my children, but they meet spring in their own ways now that they have nearly grown up.

The soil feels promising and warm in the palm of my hand. I rake away the debris of winter just as my mother did. Once, only once, a garter snake interrupted my spring cleaning. Perhaps he had somehow navigated through the streets and yards from the nearby ravine. He surprised me and brought to mind a dark-haired young woman and her young son of decades ago. With my rake I tried to steer him toward the hedgerows between yards, where he might have a chance to survive. I suppose his appearance as I was raking my garden could be called a coincidence, but I tend to believe less and less in coincidence now. Instead I see such occurrences as patterns that are simply, slowly repeated.

Chickweed and sorrel have a head start in the garden beds, and I have to pull them by hand before spading the soil. Mine is a modest garden, and its reward may lie in the planting rather than the harvest. I approach it as the rite of spring of a late-twentieth-century middle-aged man. In the first turning of soil, I unearth my wilder little neighbors with whom I share this plot. A toad now and then, or the iridescent black caterpillar-hunter beetles that struggle frantically when my spading flips them on their backs. There are moth pupae also—dark mahogany shells that remind me of mummies. I shovel them back into the soil with some misgivings, knowing that when they become caterpillars they will sample my vegetables before I do.

Each year I uncover, in nearly the same spot, a queen bumblebee. It cannot be the same bee each year, but I think of her that way. She is my sleeping beauty, her wings and black and yellow velvet bands immaculate and brilliant. Before returning her to sleep, I hold her in the hollow of my palm. Her yellow bands glisten like nuggets of captured summer sun.

I like the look of a raked garden bed just before planting; that square is my readied canvas, and I have some notion of joining the season in laying out what will be the living colors to come. I like to make furrows for the seeds with the edge of my hand, to delve the earth and let it dry in the creases of my palm. I tie strings for snow peas and beans to direct them skyward. Nesting sparrows and robins busily pick last year's twine from the piles of debris I raked between the beds. Spring invites such busyness.

This spring I plan to take time from busyness to once again sit by the river where my daughter was born. It will be a day in early May, and if it should rain I am sentimental enough to hope for a rainbow. I will sit with my wife and with many other parents and watch my daughter take her college degree. And I will listen, perhaps not with full attention, to the speakers who will speak of commencement, of beginnings. But for me, on that May day, spring will promise more than beginnings. My dark-haired daughter will hold the years to come, but she has also held my hand, as I once held the hand of a young woman in a garden so many years ago. We are joined. The circle grows but does not end: This is the covenant, the promise of spring.

Sites and Other Stories from the Past

LIKE A SECRET, THE past wants to be discovered. To the attentive, the earth in its own good time leaks tantalizing stories—glimpses and fragments of time near and far removed. The ground itself is a palimpsest, a tablet written upon, partially erased, and marked again. Not long ago I watched a bulldozer in Mehling Gulch scrape out a shallow pit for the most recent construction project on our campus. The gulch has been a landfill for years, and under the topsoil the plow blade unearthed successive layers of rubble in neat shelves of concrete, brick, and asphalt. The plow revealed that the signs of the past can be anywhere, for they lurk beneath our feet like nearly forgotten memories. Before forms were laid for the new building, the pit resembled an archaeological dig where stones and bricks are like words of a story we partially overhear, that we must reconstruct. And such stories have characters, people who once stood where we now stand. The fragments they left are reminders that we can touch as well as see. We do not have to search far to find them.

I live in an old house in an old neighborhood. When I decided to turn part of my back lawn into a vegetable garden, the elders among my neighbors were chagrinned: The back yard had always been a lawn. I ignored convention and took great care in planning my bed, even marking out my perimeter with stakes and cord. I hit rock when I turned my first spadeful of sod. Or more correctly, I hit bricks placed end to end in the ground under the string that outlined my plot. On hands and knees I stooped to remove the bricks; one by one I pulled them out and reversed the work of some other gardener, long moved away, who also fancied chrysanthemums or zucchini in that ideal patch of the yard. No one but I had held those bricks since that other weekend farmer placed them in the ground at least a generation ago. Such relics foster an odd sense of kinship.

My garden has prospered, and I have dispersed the bricks in walkways and borders about my yard. I couldn't single them out now if I had to. When I took them from the ground, mortar and soot stains intimated some earlier history as part of a wall or chimney. Like so many sites and relics, they had traveled in time without much notice or ceremony. But sometimes we do take notice and participate in ad hoc ceremonies.

May Day occasioned such a gathering in downtown Portland. As the sun rose the old Corbett Building fell. Ten thousand spectators positioned themselves like pigeons and starlings on the rooftops and window ledges of adjoining buildings to witness the event. The implosion took five seconds. Like raging fire, the collapse promised spectacle and potential danger, but I suspect the crowd's fascination had other roots as well. A rise or a fall enthralls us. Demolition and construction, destruction and creation, death and life: These are the bricks of history, pieces of the mosaic that includes us all.

Dump trucks soon carted the bricks and mortar of the Corbett Building to landfills. In a few years a new building will take its place. Such transformations seem the rule, but there are exceptions. Midway between downtown Portland and the University of Portland, Graham Street ends where it meets Interstate Avenue. Only a few buildings and trees remain as lonely sentinels in most of the nearby lots. The intersection languishes in the shade of columns and ramps; overhead the Fremont Bridge looms, a canopy of concrete. Although no building remains in the very last block of Graham Street, there is a curious and generally unobserved ruin. There is a sidewalk, a head-high retaining wall, and a solitary set of concrete stairs that leads up a hillside to an abandoned lot of waist-high grass and wildflowers. Seen at a distance the wall, stairs, and mound of greenery mimic an Egyptian mastaba or a Mayan pyramid. No Pharaoh's bones molder within the mound, but it speaks of antiquity. Its stairs lead to the past. Though unrecorded, the history of this ruin is not forgotten. For thirty-seven years Gavin Campbell, owner and proprietor of Campbell's Cleaners, has watched the evolution of the neighborhood through the lettered window of his business. He can stand in his doorway, two blocks from the ruin, and with a finger point and paint a picture of a time when a market stood here and an apartment building there. And yes, he remembers the apartment building at the top of the stairs that stood where the mound is now. "Who knows," he asks, "in five years this could all change again?" He is right, of course. There are cycles of land use. But it is not always humanity that determines the cycles.

The earth itself can decree what will stand and what will fall, what will disappear and what will be revealed. At times the natural forces exert themselves slowly and subtly. Summers in our Willamette Valley, for instance, have been dry in recent years. The shore line of Sauvie Island retreated considerably last summer and exposed a wet site, the remnants of a pre-Columbian settlement preserved in the mud of the riverbank. Where cattle used to slake their summer thirst, archaeologists now sift for artifacts—the property and household goods of the earliest residents of our valley. Carefully labeled shards and projectile points offer clues about the tribe who dwelt on this riverbank. Through archaeology we have raised our curiosity about our ancestors to an exact science. An uninformed observer encountering the stakes, strings, and shallow trench of the site could be forgiven for mistaking it for a construction project, a future building rather than the rebuilding of the past. And it is an odd and tantalizing thought that the people of this same settlement, perhaps two thousand years ago, walked on the land where the university now stands or the lot on Graham Street with the ghostly stairs or the block where the Corbett Building fell.

I searched many years ago for a site where bones as well as stones survived the years. Near Oxford, New York, I followed close upon the heels of hunters and their hounds who had discovered a small tomb erected not long after the American Revolution. The builders had immediately abandoned the tomb to the care of the forest. Local legend claimed that a family who farmed the area buried their youngest child there. This was the child's tomb, "Little Merritt's Grave," in the legend. Little Merritt feared the dark, so his people buried him atop the soft earth in a fieldstone tomb with a skylight that faced the morning sun. Some said Little Merritt's bones were still there. I hoped to see him as well as the grave, for I've always felt that the bones or fossils of our forbearers confer a special dignity on a site. Time can abstract the long dead so that the geometry and architecture of bone speak to us like a sculpture. But I did not find my way to the tomb; I never met Merritt's skeleton stare. The Irish poet Seamus Heaney, musing on a fossilized man pulled from a peat bog in Denmark, imagined that in the old Dane's presence he would "feel lost, Unhappy and at home." I expected to feel that way, too. The Dane and Little Merritt are distant kin who have preceded us in both the land of the living and the dead.

As a youngster I once pressed my face against a glass case that housed an Egyptian mummy still wrapped in the windings of its linen shroud. About the mummy's feet the wrappings had disintegrated. Three toes, brown, withered, and stone hard, protruded. They were the same size as my own toes and they frightened me. It was not the childish fright that fuels nightmares, but the fright of a harsh insight. Seeing the toes was an initiation into the world of the living and the dead. I knew then that my life had come to me from people who died long ago and that our worlds overlapped. I knew that any place could become a site and that anyone could be embedded in the earth for the future to ponder. And I know now that the story found in our remains may be as moving as the stories we find in the sites of our predecessors. For those of us inclined to celebrate that shared life and its story, a site possesses the aura of a shrine and the bone the value of a relic.

Travellers and Dwellers

TEMPERAMENT AS WELL AS the times sort out travellers and dwellers. I like to think that both may be explorers and discoverers: Those who journey and visit, those who stay and inhabit. History and literature bear witness to both of these pursuits. Lewis and Clark, Barry Lopez: Travellers. Henry David Thoreau, Annie Dillard: Dwellers. My prejudice favors the stay-at-home discoverers, and I readily admit to a long life as a resident explorer. The near-at-hand has rewarded me amply.

Over the years that I've wandered about the ninety or so acres of the university's campus, I've felt a peculiar kinship with Captain William Clark, who walked the same ground nearly two centuries ago. What caught his eye often catches mine—birds especially. In a journal entry he noted that the birds ". . . were immensely numerous, and their noise horrid." Perhaps that is not quite the case today, but birds remain a source of almost daily discovery if you are patient and watch closely from dawn 'til dusk and from season to season.

Of all the life Clark saw, the only remaining living witness to his visit on today's campus is a great white oak that spreads itself over the building that houses our bookstore. Our head groundskeeper tells me that this tree had already found its place in the sun a hundred years before Clark and his colleagues looked out on the Willamette from the nearby bluff. The oak is my monument to those past explorers and the starting point of the nearly 7,000 days that I have set foot on these acres. I, too, note the wildlife that continues to inhabit The Bluff and its environs despite the steady loss of woods and green spaces. I take what the acres give me.

The oak gives voice only through the wind, but it serves as a podium or pulpit for a flock of crows who may well be descended from the horrid noisemakers of centuries past. I am convinced that one especially evangelical among them waits every morning to deliver a scolding homily that rouses me from the remnants of my dreams and sets my day on the right path. That task done, he and his brethren wander to the woods on The Bluff where they spend most of the day in other mischief. Once in a while, I catch them at angry missions. An owl who ventured out too early or too low falls prey to the flock of crows, which pursues like an airborne street gang, chasing the slower-flying owl from tree to tree until the owl gains enough height to escape or the crows grow bored. The harried owl invites sympathy, but at worst it is his demeanor and feathers that are ruffled. I have seen crows and blue jays suffer similar harassment from nesting robins, who propel themselves into the backs and breasts of marauders with the abandonment of kamikazes. The robins are not always successful in driving off their tormentors. Pale blue shards of dropped eggs and stiff, transparent fledglings lie among the fallen blossoms and other detritus of spring.

The only cost of my stationary exploring is time stolen from my usual schedule. Perhaps the birds catch my eye because they are so free, so unattached to schedule. Raucous or regal, their very ability to fly is an enviable freedom and the most graceful face of the campus wilderness.

It is a wilderness with many faces. There are free-spirited barn swallows, streamlined birds that loop-the-loop over and about anyone who strolls the lawns that they patrol. Their huge-eyed, fearless nestlings peer from the mud nests their parents have built under campus eaves and along walkways. There are winter wrens, shy birds that rarely venture from the dark close growth of the surrounding bluff and ravines. The first bird I ever held was a winter wren that had crashed into a window and fell dying at my feet; its death was unusual punctuation in a line that appears to run on endlessly, a line I associate with life and pleasure. There are geese, far overhead, that seem nearly mystical in their adherence to old and powerful migratory forces and formations. Their celebratory honking beckons to me like distant church bells.

The most regal of our birds are the perpetually airborne red-tailed hawks that drift over the campus, as constant and predictable in their circles as celestial bodies. The only break in the hawks' disciplined routine appears to be during mating season, when courting pairs drift together and apart in overlapping rings, the birds flying low enough for me to hear their high-pitched, plaintive cries. Once I saw a hawk eye to eye: As I stood at the edge of The Bluff, he rode a current of air below me without a ruffle of wing, rising to my level, barely a few yards away, close enough so that I could see his penetrating eyes. He drifted away from me without a wingbeat until he was beyond sight, but I remember him like a phrase from a favorite poem.

The dweller's axiom is that time becomes distance. You can journey in time, watching the inevitability and surprise of change, while remaining nearly stationary. Some things can only be discovered that way. Every exploration and discovery expands our lives, ourselves. Travellers become where they go; dwellers become where they are. I believe that in some measure we are what we see and how we see. My artist father was a cloud watcher who could see the sky as a newly painted canvas each day. I have yet to acquire the patience to explore and discover a simple skyscape, but I thrill to the birds who navigate and populate the air because they are familiar, and familiarity has a way of expanding a place. I have yet to be bored by a repeated joy or beauty. So I welcome the near wild as I do a child's face.

I especially welcome the robins. In the evening, when crows and hawks and swallows have gone to roost in the pall of first dark, the robins congregate in the campus trees. Often I stand beneath the great white oak near the bookstore and listen to their last songs. The oak's latest ring, this year's growth, bears witness to this time, this year, my years. I am added, with the robins in the branches above me, to a scroll that has recorded Lewis and Clark and the "immensely numerous" birds of their time. The robins sing out their vespers, and their song takes dominion, a lullaby and dirge to each dwindling day.

An Island in the Year

BORN IN THE SHOWERS of late spring and washed away by the rains of autumn, summer floats in the year like an enchanted island, a time set apart. It is a season of expectation and of growth, a season whose lease is never long enough.

I write these words on the twenty-second day of September, the last full day of summer. I watch summer's lease expire. There have been intimations for some time now: Yellow and brown leaves, cool mornings. The weatherman predicts a frost tonight; it would be a marvelous coincidence to have a frost on the first day of autumn. Even now in middle age I conjure up an elfin Jack glazing the leaves and blacktop roads.

Walnuts have fallen in the street in front of my house and a flock of robins mingles with finches and starlings to pick at nutmeat crushed by the tires of passing cars. But these robins do not sing; mornings and evenings are marked by their silence. As usual I failed to note the day the singing ceased and my robins moved south. The ones in the road are travelers from further north, I think. My wife and daughter heard the honking of geese earlier in the week. The V passed across that patch of sky where two hawks cried a shrieking *here, here* all summer long. Those hawks are gone also, and I didn't observe their absence immediately. Like robins and hawks, the days of summer have flown by without my noticing.

Summer may possess the longest days, but they are the fleetest, and they are days crowded with feeling and sensation. Our pagan and pantheistic pasts are bolder in summer, and our calendar of feasts reflects our inability or disinclination to subdue and convert those pasts. Summer has no holy days with the power of Halloween or Hanukkah or Christmas or Easter. Pan, Prospero, and Merlin rule summer's sway.

Summer bursts about us in light and life that is dizzying and that makes all the senses squint. Tiny mirages float above August pavements, and colors bleach in unrelenting afternoon sunlight. We unbutton and allow the heat and brightness to color us. We open doors and windows; glass gives way to screen or open air. We are drawn out, and the outside world moves closer to us. The hum of mowers, children at play, laughter, argument: All float through the tolerant window screens that rebuff only the moth, the beetle, and puffs from the cottonwood trees. Summer scents, too: Cut grass, charcoal smoke, barbecued beef, and summer rain that steams on the roads and patches of ground, that wafts back to us the warm odor of earth and greenery.

All of this we have looked forward to through the darker days of winter when we lived within ourselves. Summer is a state of mind as well as a season, a hiatus cultivated and celebrated. Harkening to an earlier calendar, we release our children in the growing season. The old spell dies hard, and we persist in our longing to nurture and watch growth. The world's most basic hopes and expectations still rest on the harvest of rice, wheat, potatoes—crops. And, as always, our hopes rest in and for our children. At the end of summer the crops are harvested and we have our children stand by the door frame to put a new line marking this summer's growth.

My mother, an efficient Yankee, liked to watch her children and her garden grow at the same time. My brothers and I were not trusted with the flower beds, which were her private space and joy. But the vegetable garden, once she had planted it, became our responsibility and chore. I found no joy in the routine of watering, weeding, and picking. Since I didn't particularly care to eat much of what I tended, the garden could be an irksome chore, one that I complained about till I reached the limits of mother's bountiful patience.

Our first garden lay in the back corner of our lot, a little patch of farm land you could find then or now anywhere in this country. It survived my initial indifferent and uninspired husbandry, and it reached out with summer's green fingers to stroke and scratch me. Weeding left dirt in my nails; they always seemed longer after I found a way to scrape the dirt out. Tomato plants not only stained my fingers but also left my skin feeling fuzzy, and raspberry canes found ways to stick me no matter what contortions I employed to evade them.

I warred all summer long with weeds that could outgrow vegetables and strangle our lettuce and carrots if I gave them a couple of days' grace. And my efforts often ended up simply providing a salad course for rabbits, slugs, snails, and caterpillars, who left me ragged leaves and, in the case of the rabbits, a trail of pellet droppings. In a child's way I learned the frustration and dashed hopes of failed crops. But I also saw in the strangling weeds the voracious imperialism of the green world, whose seeds and spores colonized wherever and whenever the summer's light and moisture allowed.

That garden was my outdoor school—classroom enough to study the season and life itself. I spent a great deal of time in our garden, and when we moved to apartments and rented houses I missed my old classroom. As soon as I owned a home, I put in a garden.

The first stories in our culture are garden stories, stories of summer worlds where there are snakes, where Cains murder Abels. It was in summer and in a garden world that Cain brought us death, and his legacy has endured. Summer is death as well as growth—so much life makes for so much death. Whatever is born must feed: The spittle bug and the aphid suck life from the plant, the lacewing and ladybug devour the aphid. The morning glory chokes the shoot of the raspberry as they both struggle for a place in the sun. The tender, the young, the vulnerable are the bulk of this harvest. Crows pick clean the small carcasses that spot summer roads; fledglings fall from nests to dry up on sidewalks in the square of hopscotch games. More die than live.

Usually such deaths are impersonal, but there are ancient enmities that resemble the clashes of human clans, and there are chance encounters that provoke unexpected violence. Early this summer I heard a blue jay screaming in the street, and I assumed he had spotted a crow. When I looked over my fence, however, I saw the jay stabbing with his beak at a small animal that scooted about in an erratic and panicked frenzy. It was a mole; burrowing along the earth between sidewalk and street, it must have fallen over the curb and into the street, which became an unscalable canyon for the little creature.

I moved in and the jay moved off. But the mole was too large to hold bare-handed, and I soon as I moved away the jay attacked it; the bird's blood lust was stronger than his fear of me. Eventually I ran for a shovel and scooped the mole into a clump of high weeds by the fence. His brown fur was silky and shiny, almost black, but the jay had opened a hole in his side and his life oozed out. He would not survive. Ordinarily mole and jay inhabit different realms: One a creature of earth and night, the other of air and day. Perhaps it was the breaking of this pattern that startled the bird into what seemed wanton violence.

In my early summers I, too, had my days of Cain, and I swallowed the bitter aftertaste of my own wanton violence more than once. I remember walking barefoot with other boys in and along a brook that crossed several pastures near my home. Here and there the water opened into waist-deep pools. Small brook trout darted in these pools, and my companions and I sharpened willow saplings into short spears. We pierced our own reflections trying to stab the fish. We bombed the pools with stones, driving the fish into streamlets where they foundered in the shallow water. We took them then with rocks and spears. Had we intended to eat them, the experience would have had a different taste. But we weren't fishermen, and we plied a very different trade. It was work that took me closer to nature than I had intended and its intimations disturbed me.

When I was twelve, my parents put me on a train and shipped me off to my aunt's house for the summer. This happened for the next four years. It was something of a family tradition: My aunt's only child was grown, and he had spent his summers with my folks. So off I went to the aptly named town of Pleasantville to live in a glass-walled house designed by a student of Frank Lloyd Wright, a house set apart from neighbors in the country.

My aunt must have been considered an eccentric back then, in the 1950s, though she would seem rather "with it" now. She espoused health food, practiced a forthright ecumenism, read *The Catholic Worker*, disdained lawns, knew by sight every wildflower in Westchester County, and favored slacks, work boots, and turtleneck jerseys. She possessed a splendid soprano and was a regular in her church choir and a Bach group. She loved animals, was an awful cook, and treated me as an equal.

We suited each other. We wandered her acres; she with a trowel to transplant some prized wildflower or herb closer to her house, I with a jar and net, ever-watchful for a beetle or moth. Perhaps I was a blooming eccentric too. At night we would sit in the darkness by the glass walls and watch the congress of insects drawn from the surrounding woods by the exterior lights. We had a window into the nocturnal world, and we sat as if by a watering hole in the wilderness. The pages of my insect field guides came alive across the window panes. June bugs and longhorn beetles bounced against the glass like walnuts; luna moths floated out of the darkness as pale, delicate ghosts. At the edges of the light, predators like the mantis went about their business, and it was a great harvest for the spiders that had placed their webs like fish nets in the bay of light. But death remained on the periphery. The light precipitated and illuminated a frenzy of courting, mating, and egg laying, and my aunt and I watched in fascination.

In miniature the spectacle of life and death played before us on the glass. In the morning I would find discarded insect legs and wings under the spider webs, and clusters of eggs, each no larger than a pinhead. I learned the facts of life and death at my aunt's elbow, though it remained for a long time a knowledge understood rather than felt. My curiosity about the out-of-doors was insatiable, but I remained an observer, a watcher. My innocence remained like panes of glass between me and the world that I imagined outside of me.

But I soon learned otherwise—again at my aunt's elbow. During rainy days we would dress up and go into New York City with my uncle. Our usual plan was to have lunch with him and then explore the Museum of Natural History. Two halls per outing was our routine, and it was in these halls, where nature was fixed in an unchanging summer, that the panes of innocence began to break. The first crack appeared in the Hall of Man.

Along the walls of the hall, cross-sections of human reproductive organs were arranged to illustrate the differences in males and females, and to reveal the growth of a human child from egg and sperm cells to birthing child. The plaster models, life-like in color and detail, interested me in the same way the stuffed animals did or the exhibits of Egyptian and Mayan burial customs. But my aunt paused long and reverently before the model of an embryo in its third month.

"I lost two just like that," she said. "Two little ones." She whispered the sentence again, fondly and sadly, and she remained at the glass case like a mourner at a grave.

I left her and wandered alone into the next hall, where low display cases served as a railing that overlooked an immense white bowl as large as a swimming pool. The cases held framed butterflies and moths whose wings shimmered under fluorescent light. Wings from every known habitat lipped the great bowl where a life-sized whale floated serenely in a sea of air, a womb carried on the wings of butterflies. And I knew then, as the mournful woman I had left a moment ago had known all along, that the hall of man is not really a separate room. We may choose to observe, but we must experience. Birth, growth, and death claim all of us, woman and boy as well as butterfly and whale.

That was a long time ago, and yet another summer has slipped through my fingers. At the season's passing I pull this memory of my aunt from the streambed of remembrance; it is a moment saved from the torrent of impressions and experiences. Two other moments from the hearts of summers I also save: One a memory of my father, the other of my son.

I hiked once with my father along old stone walls that edged the fields where he schooled horses for a neighbor. We took refuge from the day's heat by slipping beneath the arms of the spruce and hemlock trees that fringed the adjoining woods. He took me to a stream that drained from the hills and cascaded over a small falls into a deep pool. It was the summer of my growth spurt, when I felt long and awkward. The cold of the pool stung me for my trespass, but I submerged, frog-style, and examined the pebbles on the bottom through water clear as glass. My father sat at the pool's edge and allowed the stream to bathe his bare feet. He said nothing. He just watched me and pondered, to a depth beyond my experience or intuition.

I sat this summer in the stands of a long-course swimming pool waiting for my son to compete in a race. The day was hot and without the shade of spruce and hemlock trees. I peered out under the shadow of my hand as my son mounted the starting block. I marked my son, saw the line of my bones in his bones. His bones were longer, leaner. He was young and I am becoming old. I marked him well, and along with him I held my breath as he exploded into the water. My mind plunged to an unexpected depth until he surfaced to swim, with power and grace, in a lane that was his alone. With expectation, with gratitude, I watched him pull away, taking me with him, forever leaving me behind.

I See, I See

I SEE, I SEE, WHAT do you see? Summer. Our movements set the hammock to gentle swinging. We float together, a father and a daughter, like the proverbial peas but in a green canvas pod. I do not answer her question immediately. I would rather float with her in silence; when you can no longer be held as a child, you hold a child. I would hold her, the moment, against the past or the future. She persists. I answer.

I see, I see, what do you see? I see something green high in the sky. Somewhere, someone knows the rules to the game. I have lost them, perhaps with my childhood. What I remember suffices, has made do for my three children who have grown in and out of the game as I have simply grown older. The game has become a pattern and it is the pattern of my life. As a teacher I answer questions, share what I have seen. Every father, every mother, is teacher to their child; every teacher becomes, whether he wishes or not, something of a parent to his students. An arguable point for many, but on a summer day a truth I accept for myself. During the academic year other fathers and mothers lend me their sons and daughters.

They sit, these other people's children, in neat rows before me, ready to commit my wisdom to spiral pad; or better yet, I sit with them in the best seminar fashion, like a family 'round the kitchen table. We look at our shared texts through the steam rising from styrofoam cups of coffee and tea. To a certain cast of mind, the whole procedure may seem as insubstantial as a hammock. The thought has occurred to me. Can the future really depend on scraps of words marked with pink and yellow hilighter pens in cheaply made paperbacks? On the questions of well-fed innocents? On the musings of a middle-aged professor who has never dramatically experienced war, poverty, or injustice? Apparently it can. Magically, gracefully, we are often best as teachers, as parents, when we are least aware, often in a comment or gesture that we never anticipated in the syllabus. Our success or failure may often rest on our unremembered acts. One does what one can. And the future unfolds on the strength of the questions that our children ask. Often inarticulate, clumsy, irreverent—the questions remain a moral force that elevates our tutelage beyond the banality suggested by the stains of coffee rings on a seminar table and the scribbled marginalia in a textbook. These may finally signify not only the passage of time but also of knowledge.

In the hammock and in the class, the young ask what I see. What are the great questions? What are the answers? One question is war. One answer is peace. Why one more in the world and not the other? The mystery perplexes. I feel the young cannot see the world as it is. They want insight as well as sight, but I am no prophet. I have no new eyes to give, only my tired vision and the afterimages of the literature that I have taught over the years. Nonetheless, I chart a course through the world of literature. Through Tolstoy and Conrad and Golding and Pasternak and Paton and Gordimer and Wiesel. This game is new to my students, and I am still very much in control. What have I given in these forays into art and into the near and remote past? A glimpse of the heart of darkness? I cannot lead them back into history and myth without regret, and I force them (gently, for we seem at first to be talking more of books, more of paper people, than of life, of our lives) to glance over their shoulders. I invite them to see the horrors. None is turned to salt. But we have faced the darkness. We have acknowledged injustice.

I see, I see a leaf. What do you see? It would be easy to ignore thoughts of peace and justice. It would be especially easy during a calm season where time and distance conspire to blur the cruelties that are always closer than we think. I would rather hear the voice of my child and feel the sway of the hammock. I would rather celebrate the good and forget the evil. Yet celebration balances but does not obliterate darkness. We must acknowledge both. And so we hold our children in love and protection; in the world in which we live the gestures are nearly synonymous. Parents hold children as poets hold the world: As treasures at once valuable and vulnerable. I do not believe this to be mere sentimentality. We should celebrate the truly valuable and vulnerable. If ever I proselytize, it will be in the name of the writers who have such a vision of the world.

For me Boris Pasternak comes closest to realizing this vision, and it is to his work that I most often turn and most often lead my students. His Zhivago, the poet and doctor, writes poems by candlelight while Lara and her little girl sleep, while wolves prowl outside, while the great war and the great revolution swirl outside his window like the cruel Russian winter.

In his lonely vigil Zhivago is the good and just man for our time, a hope for our era. Would that his thoughts could be our thoughts: "As he scribbled his odds and ends, he made a note reaffirming his belief that art always serves beauty, and beauty is delight in form, and form is the key to organic life, since no living thing can exist without it, so that every work of art, including tragedy, expresses the joy of existence." What do I see here? What would I have my students or my grown children see? No more than the "odds and ends" of literature (and the odds and ends of life) that "express the joy of existence." I would have them sense what Pasternak has Zhivago and Lara feel: "And why is it . . . that my fate is to see everything and take it all so much to heart?" I would have them see, celebrate, and balance the light and the darkness.

And as I swing on my hammock and ponder, I cannot hide a certain distaste for the politics and ideologies that inevitably discolor such reflections. At best I have found them necessary evils and have had to face the accusation of cowardice for retreating from the issues of the day. I would rather turn over the soil of the raised beds in my garden than march on federal buildings for peace. An activist philosopher whose friendship I lost over this issue saw my garden beds as burial mounds dug by apathy or indifference. It is not an easy accusation to dismiss. Perhaps he feels enough to see things more clearly than I do. I fear sometimes that he does. But other times I feel the resistance to activism is not inertia but a counter-force that would have me turn my garden, hold my daughter, teach my books, live and love close to the earth. I hear in this a friendly echo of another great Russian. The dramatist and short story writer, Checkov, believed that "if every man did what he could on his little bit of soil, how marvelous our world would be." If the world tended its garden, held its children closely, what a different world it might be. The ideal speculations of a summer's afternoon? The mere reflections of a man on a hammock? Yet the reluctance to shoulder a protest poster may spring from the same reluctance to shoulder a rifle. Undoubtedly there is a time for both of these—the rifle and the poster—and for my daughter and my students I do not presume how they should choose. I have only "odds and ends" to share, and their questions may teach me more than my answers teach them. Together we try to see.

Before all else we must see. The hope for peace and justice rests with this simple truth. And we do live in hope. The child and the poem, children and literature, are predicated on a belief in the future as well as a celebration of the present.

This was my discovery when as a college student I listened to one of my teachers read from a book of his poems. The poet was Daniel Berrigan, Father Daniel Berrigan, who sometime later would become famous for his resistance to the Vietnam conflict. We were both younger then: I the age of my present students; he a teacher the age I am now. We were joined, however, by his words, which he recited quietly, almost in a whisper, so that I felt myself leaning toward him so as to miss nothing. And since the war had not yet begun, he did not speak of "peace making" being "hard almost as war" but of hope like a cricket who responds to

> *. . . miniscule dawn*
> *match flare might make, or candle end*
> *and he foolish cry dawn! at the*
> *false dawn*
> *that wakened him for death.*
> *How small a thing is hope*
> *hairspring body, mind's eye, and all*
> *endangered.*

Hope nonetheless. I too would cry dawn and would keep faith with the poets who first see it. And in their company I hold the small body of my daughter and continue:

I see, I see, what do you see?

The Poignant Season

THE MIND IS A GENTLE and poetic editor, and the loops and circles of association rework events. So for me autumn memories are like the piles of leaves that I raked with my father and brothers years ago: Nothing is lost, but each caress of the prongs spreads the red maple leaves, the yellow elm, and the brown oak into a different pattern of shapes and hues.

I have my mother's word that I was born in winter during a severe snowstorm, severe even by the New England reckoning of our neighbors. But that storm and the Pittsfield, Massachusetts, streets it buried belong to my mother's memory; I only remember her stories. So much of my childhood is that way: Memories of things told rather than lived. And much of what *was* lived is jumbled events that leap and flash like trout in sunlight before they disappear back into dark water.

My first five years were the years of my first childhood, a childhood of summer, a childhood of body time: Time for the eye and hand, time to run. Like the sun, summer left its mark on me: Grass stain, grasshopper juice, foam of spittle bugs, crushed strawberries.

Those summers ended on the last Sunday evening before my first year at school began. On that night, every year from that time on, my brothers and I would come in from the early dark, still sweating from some glorious chase, and the cool of the house would almost chill us. The grass and the nettles that we had trampled would now blotch and sting us in revenge. After our baths my father would stand each of us against the white enameled door frame of the kitchen pantry. With a pencil he marked our heights and the date. The marks were our bodies' report cards; summer had belonged to the body, but on Monday we would learn to sit, to be still.

The autumn of my fifth year swims in the shallows of memory, and I can grab it, the first fingerling in the school of fifty autumns that measure my days. When my mother took me by the hand to Notre Dame Grammar School, I left my summer childhood behind. Had she not held me, I would have run back to fireflies and cap pistols and wading in the Housatonic River, but she held fast and released me into halls and rooms I remember as large and redolent of ink, Pine-Sol, and our new speckled corduroys.

Sun poured through the school windows that autumn, before the rains came and before the snow. The green of summer burned off as I sat at my desk with ink-stained fingers. Bent over my desk I learned to wade in the waters of language and to trace my letters. Like all before who crouched over readers and columns of numbers, I found my thoughts racing through a different field than I had known, and I came home tired not with the familiar tiredness of hard play, or of difficult chores, but with a new and not entirely unpleasant ache. I brought my books for the year home in those first autumn days, and they smelled as new as my new leather school shoes. My father cut covers from grocery sacks and bound the folds and spines with wide masking tape. In time I would cover my own books, an act that marked growing-up as definitely as the height markers on the pantry door frame. At night as the old elm that stooped over our house began to shed, I leafed through my new books, impatient and excited by what lay ahead.

I did not know then that time had changed for me and my friends, that no more would we run bare-chested through sprinklers, or swim in the stony-bottomed, spring-fed lakes with Indian names—Onota, Pontoosuc—or play baseball in the vacant lot behind our homes. Instead we would swim naked and embarrassed at the Y and shoot hoops in the CYO gym, where the walls would throw our shouts and screams back at us. In summer fields our cries had traveled forever, but now migrating monarch butterflies cruised through the golden fields, and the surviving swallowtails and sulphurs of early summer limped in the breeze on tattered wings and missing legs.

Autumn had its own treasures, however, even if our time for finding them was short. Pine cones littered the carpet of needles in the woods behind our parish church, and we would fire them at each other though they did not carry very far; it was battle-practice for the serious snowballing of the season to come. We filled our pockets with acorns and horse chestnuts, the smooth shiny surfaces of which looked like the burl of polished hardwoods. It felt good to rub them on our cheeks, to feel the smoothness pass over the skin between our nose and lips. We would cut out their centers and insert twigs, thereby fashioning pipes that would eventually shrivel on our windowsills and bookshelves.

Unaware, we also gathered burdocks and burrs and thistledown which rode the cuffs of our corduroys. Farmers plant in spring, but the green world sows in the fall. Each fall we were sowers out-of-doors but fallow fields in the classroom, where we sat in expectant rows, each of us a furrow for whatever our teachers, brilliant or bad, cast among us. Much fell on good ground, but wildflowers flourished too, and up sprouted thoughts and notions uniquely beautiful and prickly like thistle and teasel and bindweed. No two rows grew alike.

Out-of-doors was a book for reading and learning also, and we closely studied the dramatic changes of autumn, when one can almost feel a motion in the earth. Winds blew harder in the darkening afternoons, and we let ourselves be carried about like thistledown and cattail-fluff. In orchards we pitched and batted the last windfall apples and pears, sharing the wormy fruit with robins who got drunk on the overripe harvest and flew away erratically. The robins sneaked away, one by one, until one day you realized that they were all gone. But the starlings remained, descending on the lines of poplars, their great flocks blackening the grey skies above us. While individual starlings are rather shabby residents in the city of air, their flocks veer and undulate with inexplicable grace and unison, a visual symphony of harmonious motion.

But it is only in memory that those flocks were things of beauty. Our compulsion then was something deeper and darker. As our fathers and uncles took out shotguns and deer rifles to bag pheasant and whitetail, so we took our BB guns and homemade bows and stalked the enormous flocks of starlings. Wild boys we were and the starlings rightful prey, a great bounty of earth subject to our power and violence. Perhaps this was our first flush of lust: To see and feel the thousands flee in confusion at our shouts excited us. We shot our arrows without aiming, and what we dropped was the victim of improbability rather than skill. For most of us the chase was short-lived and left behind without reflection or regret, but some pursued it long.

As darkness grew longer, we ventured out with the neighborhood's blessing as witches, skeletons, monsters, clowns, black-hatted pilgrims. Paper sacks in hand, we retraced the same streets where we gathered chestnuts and acorns, but this time we plied our cuteness and innocence to add to our hoard of candy corn, Hershey Kisses, and the odd pennies and nickels dispensed by gentlemen retirees. The coins sank to the bottoms of our bags and clinked like change in the pockets of those same venerable gentlemen. We grew bolder with the passing of years and moved more easily with the darkness, staring at the night world through the slit eye-holes of masks. Between the flashes of light from opened doors we breathed back our child-breath behind the masks, but felt larger than children in the security of our costumes. Without notion of religion, myth, or history, we romped and thrilled in our ancient ritual, tricking or treating.

But the depth and shades of autumn dark did not entirely elude us. Real pilgrims had walked the streets of my hometown, and after them Melville and Hawthorne; for many years people had slept uneasily there, thinking that real witches walked among them. Somehow the dark hand of the past rested heavy on the little town of my youth, even though the world seemed so much safer then.

One odd permutation of this darkness was a huge *papier-mache* pumpkin, taller than a man, which was placed on a platform in the center of town every October. It sat there like a great deity of the harvest: Rotund, menacing, demanding. Another was the dragon that incongruously brought up the end of my city's October 31st parade of school bands and floats. The dragon's name was Pitt, and he had been built in the early 1950s by the General Electric workers who had succeeded the textile millers as our local work force. Pitt was supposed to represent the city, somehow; Pittsfield, Pitt's field.

I do not know who among our city's fathers first imagined the dragon and the parade, but the dragon has never left my imagination. Long ago we moved away. The pumpkin burned sometime after. General Electric followed the textile mills to the cheaper South. But Pitt, who was once real and a terror to me, remains a block long and snorting steam, and he still comes round the circle and proceeds forever up North Street in my mind. I am not sure if Pitt comes to me as a visitation of the past or of the future.

My church was St. Mark's on West Street, where I knelt as an altar boy on All Saints and All Souls Days. Mornings and evenings wore the seasonal chill, and I felt my first cold intimations of mortality kneeling there in the church's shadows. Death was no stranger: I had been to the wakes of distant relatives, occasions that smelled of too many flowers, that hummed with an undercurrent of adult whispers. And as altar boy I had accompanied priest and coffin to the cemetery and looked into other people's graves. I was a bystander then, immune in my clerical costume of cassock and surplice, and safely hidden behind the mask of youth.

Death always visited in autumn, it seemed, and one autumn death in particular haunts me. It came in the November of my last year of college. The Jesuit priest who taught us psychology began his class that day with the announcement that our president had been shot.

I carry, as everyone must, the images that have become historical. But what gave me a sense of history that day wasn't an image. It was the silence that fell over the city. In the first hours of tragedy, the entire world wore shock. There were no masks; I could read my own feelings in the faces of everyone I saw. I had a sense then of connection; I felt the terrible intricacy of events and emotions spread over time and space. I had heard my parents talk of the Great Depression, of the War, of FDR; heard them speak of these grand things as if they were neighbors, familiar and personal. I had no sense then that more than a young president would be buried in the coming years, that "the times were a-changing," as Bob Dylan's song would soon proclaim. Politics would never be the same in America, nor would my notion of country. Years before Kennedy died I had collected I LIKE IKE and JFK buttons as I had collected horse chestnuts. But now I felt both the grandeur and frailty of the nation's life, and the flags and bunting of red, white, and blue evoked pity as well as pride.

In another November my father fell quietly into the past after a long and painful struggle. We buried him on a cold, rainy day that felt like winter. Other altar boys stood where I once stood; they had replaced me. They paused next to the open grave, formal and remote behind their masks of ceremony and youth.

In the last weeks of my father's life, as I sat by his bed and idly looked out a window at a horizon he could no longer see, waves of starlings passed. An undulating line seemingly without end stretched across the distant sky. I willed that they would fly over the burial day. I wished that I was a boy, and that I could run outside and watch them flee from me. And I wished that the heavens would respond to my cry one more time.

It is memory that cures, not time. The impetus of memory is to save, to preserve. The soul is a good doctor, and I believe we heal ourselves by remembering.

Shapes come back to me from my many autumns, and they come back in different hues. I see a young boy running through piles of dry leaves, the leaves flying around his ankles and knees, reaching out to trip him just as his brothers sometimes did. I see him falling from his run into a red, yellow, and brown mound of leaves. He lets the mound cover him, even his face. It is not very dark there and it smells of earth and it feels good. I see the older boy running cross country. There was play in the training, I remember. Perhaps we steal back a child's body and bodily pleasure, buy back our first summers, in our autumn games. What I recall now is not the crack of the starter's gun, or the panting of a competitor at my shoulder. Instead I hear the leaves underfoot. I smell grass becoming hay. I frighten a pheasant in that high grass; his startled squawk and flight in turn frightens me. The brief rush of adrenaline accelerates my stride, thrills me. So too does the woolly-bear caterpillar that ventures across the dusty path. He crosses my path like an unexpected memory, and then becomes a memory himself.

Autumn, fall: No other season bears two names. Perhaps it is the fullness of this season, the enormity of its harvesting and nature's planting, that calls for a double appellation. I mourn in autumn, but I also married in the fall. At the beginning and end of life our memories are closed, but the middle is open and can be shared. We may share our lives, our remembrances. Joy, pain, healing: Of these we can give and take. And many of us do just that, seated together round the harvest table, feasting in thanks and shared tales.

By then nearly all the leaves have fallen, and there is, perhaps, one more day of raking. Beneath the trees the piles of leaves seem small compared to the summer foliage that shaded entire houses. The naked branches are insubstantial and skeletal. I rake, thinking of these last leaves. Like thoughts and memories, they are the remnants of a branched whole. The last tidying passes of my rake uncover the bottom edge of the leaf pile. Already earthworms are at work, and from cracked skins of chestnuts pale rootlets reach out like curved fingers to spring.

We are Touched by Voices

HAD MUSICIANS BEEN warming up for a symphony, I would have looked down at them from my seat in this precipitously sloped and crowded balcony with an odd bird's-eye view of heads and shoulders. The stage of the concert hall was bare, however, except for a single lectern, which awaited the writer who was about to address this audience of several hundred. I closed my eyes. Instead of listening to the tuning of instruments—my more habitual ritual in this hall—I let myself be carried by the voices that I heard.

This was an orderly but noisy gathering, and the acoustics of the huge hall favored the general din. What I heard was similar to the sound of cascading, falling, rushing water. If I listened very carefully, a word or phrase would float up, without context, like a piece of driftwood. I opened my eyes when the house lights dimmed and silence settled over the hall.

The writer carried her renown on shoulders bent slightly with age. Her somber dark dress, her braided hair, her accented voice—halted somewhat by the onset of a cold—bespoke a humble presence. Here was a small old woman. But then her tenuous voice began to reach out, and the gathered hundreds bent forward as one to listen.

That solitary voice, fragile as a shore bird, pressed upon my mind with as much power as the din of hundreds. And I thought, as I followed the flight and the wisdom of that voice, how I have lived always on the shore of voices, a shore of words and sound. Like a man who has lived his entire life by the sea, I have accepted the tides and the songs of seabirds faithfully but often without thought. But the old woman behind the lectern made me hear the way of saying as well as the words said.

I thought back to the world that was merely sound before I understood my first words, my much-abridged dictionary of life. If I had to pull sounds and words from the depth of the past, they would most likely be the music and lyrics of the dawns and evenings of those early days and nights. I woke to the muffled sounds of my parents in the kitchen, sounds as inviting and delicious to me as the smell of toast, eggs, and bacon. At night, after I had made my way up the wooden hill of stairs, and my parents had tucked me in with a story or a simple "good night," I would fall asleep comforted by their voices rising from the kitchen below, sounds that brightened the dark of a child's room and his first sleep.

But sounds of family discord also rose from below, harsh words that enlarged my sense of the world and foretold the nuances of pain that we also experience. These sounds came back to me as the old woman spoke of the larger world that had been her province. And I thought of the collective voices in the provinces of my narrower experience.

I did not witness, as she did, the violence of Africa, England, and Ireland, but I knew the sounds of violence on a different scale and in a different dialect. I've known them for a long time. They were the sounds and voices in the corner of a school yard, where a circle of boys tightened around a core of hatred; in the center of that circle two boys angry beyond words flailed at each other while the circle cheered. They were the sounds of my college years when "hardhats" and "longhairs" faced each other over barricades at the entrances to universities. They are the constant sounds of anger that circle and reappear, over and over.

But the writer did not dwell on the voices of violence, and neither did I. There were and are other provinces, other voices. The rowdy cries of joy as we poured from our classrooms into the recess school yard; the rhythmic repetitions of classroom recitations; the echoes of "rover, red rover, come over" late into summer nights—these were sounds of another province. As were the cheers and boos, *ahs* and *ohs* of a stadium crowd; the collective gasps, jeers, and hurrahs in the friendly dark of the movie theater; the chants of affirmation at rallies and speeches; the great hosannas and amens of our liturgies. In all of these, words and sounds merge with a force that seems capable of shaking the heavens; the force of a people giving voice as one.

The old writer spoke into the night, one voice. And I listened, as I have throughout my life. It was the familiar and defining pattern of talk: We speak, we listen. So often I have walked down the corridors of the university lecture halls where I teach—where I, too, lecture—and from the opened or half-opened doors I hear a pastiche of knowledge and wisdom literally floating in the air.

We listen, we speak. In my office desk, along with my own lecture notes, I have saved handwritten notebooks from courses that were important to me when I was a student and listener. From time to time I reread my own scrawled writing, although I have done so enough times now to know the words nearly by heart. But I am not really reading; I am listening. For what comes through my bifocals are not words but voices. The words become their original speakers, faces reappear, past is momentarily present, in the same way that I hear voices when I read the letters and stare at the family albums in my desk at home.

Most of all we are touched by the voices of the ones we love. I sat one night, in the circle of light shed by a single lamp, reading and hearing in my mind the voice of a poet I was to teach the next day. Above, my family slept, or so I thought. An almost inaudible melody, nearly lost in the hum of the refrigerator and growl of the furnace, troubled my concentration, as the sound of a mouse in the attic or summer's last cricket might. I stalked the sound first to the staircase; then to the upper floor; then to the closed door of my youngest daughter's bedroom. In the dark she sang to herself parts of all the lyrics she knew. She was singing a medley of Christmas carols. I did not speak, only listened. Then I left her to her peaceful dark and took her music with me down the wooden hill of stairs.

When the waves of applause died down and the old writer surrendered the concert hall to the sounds of the departing crowd, I descended the balcony stairs to the lobby and walked out into the night. All the voices of the streets passed me by and flowed to destinations beyond my concern or caring. My mind was crowded with voices, but I was listening only to the words of an old woman and the songs of a girl.

Among Insects

MY COLLEAGUE, A professor of sociology, swaps stories with me. We have done this for a long time, shuffling through our experiences like boys with hands full of rubber-banded baseball cards. This time he tells me about his boyhood, but it has nothing to do with sports or our other usual swaps; rather it is a story about butterflies.

At the same age, on opposite sides of the country, the two of us had explored and hunted in the region that the naturalist Edwin Way Teale calls "grassroot jungles." Armed with wide-mouthed jars, we walked the scrub lots of our suburban youths. In his lot, an open space in a Los Angeles housing development, he captured butterflies. He was fascinated, I suppose, by their beauty and also by the temptation they pose: They can be captured by the patient and quickhanded. He made many trips to the lot, each time bringing back a butterfly in a jar. He set the jars on a windowsill in the family garage.

He watched the butterflies as they fluttered or paused to take the sun through the double panes of window and jar. They slowly opened and closed their wings like miniature oriental fans. One day his father discovered the jars and ordered an immediate release. "It was the right thing to do," says my colleague now. "Wild creatures need to be free. You don't want to be cruel. And, after all, they're better off, and happier, in their natural home."

Under the approving eyes of his father, the boy freed his prizes one by one, saving for last a jar holding his special favorite. My colleague is a big man, but as he tells his story he scrunches down in his chair and looks up with the eyes of a youth. I watch with him as his beautiful butterfly floats up into the sky—where a bird snatches it with an audible snap of its beak and eats it.

My colleague suddenly sits up, throws out his arms, and says to me the sentence he was afraid to scream at his father: "What the hell am I supposed to make of *that?*"

A good question. I think of telling him that his years of studying anomalous and bizarre subcultures in American society are probably rooted in that gobbled butterfly. But I don't. We shuffle pasts and swap more stories. Yet his anecdote pesters me like a gnat.

I have stories of my own. Last fall my family gathered in a Seattle cemetery to bury my mother. In somber clothes we stood on the garish artificial turf that hid the grave and the piled earth. The gravedigger was a careless housekeeper; raw dirt spilled out from a corner of the rug. Rain had fallen earlier in the morning, and the wet grass dampened our shoes.

An Irish priest intoned the words of the liturgy, praying for the living and the dead. His words did not fill the hollow of my grief; they were but a soft Gaelic drone in an expanded moment that had become unworldly. Then a second drone harmonized with the sounds of the liturgy. For reasons of its own a yellowjacket wasp joined our circle of mourning, making his own smaller circles in our midst. A wasp does not distinguish between park or cemetery, family picnic or funeral. He wandered among us with the indifference of absolute wildness. The priest prayed on, but the wasp had imposed himself upon the scene. Feet shuffled as he buzzed our water-stained shoes.

With instinctive disregard for ceremony and death, the wasp hovered over the polished wood of the coffin, its sprig of flowers, its metal crucifix. Then, without apology, he took his leave, and I traced his random flight above the grass and among the mute monuments. I lost sight of him, saw instead gravediggers and their machinery busy in the manicured distance, and heard the "Amen" of the liturgy. The priest took the crucifix from the coffin and gave it to my middle brother who, in turn, gave it to me, the eldest son. My hand closed on the cold metal, but the hollow of my grief was warmed by that other cross: The outstretched translucent wings and the bright yellow-and-black body of the meddling wasp.

And I wondered what to make of that.

In my time I have often witnessed the rituals of insects. A majestic old elm rose from the grassroot jungles near my boyhood home. On the elm's base I found the paper-thin shells of cicadas where they had emerged from the earth in which they grubbed as nymphs, the cicada's immature stage. The adults would spend their life among the high branches of trees, taking the day shift as summer's musicians until crickets and katydids replaced them at nightfall. I had never seen a nymph emerge, nor had I ever spotted adults, even when I could hear them buzzing above me.

But one day, by luck, I happened upon a nymph just tunneling up from the soil near the roots of the elm, and I decided to sit and bear witness to the emergence of an adult from the body of a youth.

The nymph waited, firmly attached to the bark of the tree, until the rich brown dirt encrusting its hunched back dried. I waited with it. When its back split open the adult within pulled itself out into the air. Perched on its past, it teetered slightly as its transparent wings unfolded and dried. My presence was so gargantuan, I believe, that I did not register in its consciousness. Eventually it spread its wings and flew off to go forth and multiply. All that remained was the husk of its shell, and my wonderment at this curious transformation.

The time for cicadas is a season away, but the unexpected warmth of spring foreshadows late summer. Yesterday I sat on my back stairs, under the miniature leaves of a budding lilac. From a crack in the foundation of my house a relentless line of ants streamed forth; winged males took to the air. I had to wave my hands before my face to keep them from my eyes and nostrils. Today it rained; the only winged ants that survived the day of flight and mating are the ones that hijacked a ride into my room by landing on my clothing. A few dance on my window pane; others find their way to the pages I am writing. They wander about like displaced letters. Every year I spray that crack with Raid, and every year the ants return. Their progeny will outlive mine.

I wonder what to make of this also.

Ants, cicadas, wasps, butterflies—they are enigmatic little poems. It is no accident that those people who notice them are blessed with almost mystical nearsightedness: Poets, scientists, children. Nor is it an accident that we become poets, scientists, and children when we are momentarily arrested by the beauty and strangeness of these creatures. They are so small, their kingdom so vast.

Between Wars

MY SELECTIVE SERVICE notification arrived during the happy days long after Korea and before Vietnam. Like a driver's license, the registration card conferred a certain *gravitas* on the thin plastic card-and-photo holder of my wallet and my even thinner self. It was something to show the girls.

Again we are between wars, and my only son received his Selective Service notification a year ago. I'm not sure how young men view this rite of passage today, but as a father I now watch the years ahead with anxiety and look back and ponder a past that has sent some men to war and left others home to later hear their stories. Two entirely different paths diverge, both mapped by the unpredictable motions of history and a man's birth date. Chance, hazard, the luck of the draw.

Neither I nor my father went off to war. My French grandfather did. My father wanted to be a soldier and couldn't: He was too old for World War II. I wasn't sure if I wanted to be a soldier in Vietnam, but I was just old enough that I didn't have to make a decision. The war passed me by. I faced no crisis of conscience. I believe poverty rather than politics or patriotism motivated grandfather: Soldiering in North Africa and Indochina had to be more inviting that the slums of Marseilles.

My grandfather died before my birth, and his stories came to me second hand by way of my romantic father, who told them with awe and nostalgia. I am convinced grandfather used his past to season the present in a rather casual and anecdotal way. I remember cutting my right palm when I was quite young in the days of stinging iodine and Mercurochrome. As my father painted the cut, he retold one of his father's stories. During a battle in North Africa, grandfather had been wounded in the same hand. During the heat of the engagement he couldn't get proper antiseptic, so he staunched the wound with the only thing available—pepper. My uncle told me the same story years later when I cut my hand while on a summer's visit. He told the story, word for word, his voice rising and falling just as my father's had, just as their father's must have when he dressed their cuts.

This and other retold stories have passed into family lore, and from them emerges a man touched deeply by many experiences; war was one of them, bootlegging another. I believe grandfather took life as it came, perhaps with detachment and always with an eye open to irony and earthy humor. Pepper more than the pitch of battle got passed to the next generations.

It was my father who added a tone, or perhaps just a note, that did not quite fit what I felt was grandfather's original score. There was shading in the retelling, something almost unnoticeable. It was more apparent when my father retold war stories he heard from men of his own generation: Men he worked with at General Electric, his buddies on the YMCA pistol team, a neighbor. He did not seek the stories; they simply came his way. But there was a kind of sadness or regret in his retelling, a tension I felt but could not understand.

In high school and my first years of college, teachers and coaches spoke of the war. So I began to hear about soldiering without my father as intermediary. Like grandfather's stories theirs also sprung from the present, from the casual and ordinary. Yet what they described was truly past to me. I remember sitting at the kitchen table with my track coach and his family. Sometimes after a late workout he would take me home for dinner and I would sit between his two youngest children. The rare war stories my coach told were real enough, but I found it difficult to see him in them, to see him as a young man my age. His greying hair and paunch did not match the movie images that were my frame of reference. On a side table in my coach's living room was a double picture frame. In one panel a picture of him in uniform, in the other his purple heart. They seemed museum pieces.

My father and I both watched Vietnam from the sidelines. And for both of us it was a confusing war, though perhaps for different reasons. We talked little, for our words always became cross. In this we were no different from many other fathers and sons, but it was painful for us.

Boys I went to school with, guys who shared summer evenings playing rat ball at the hoops in the park, the kid next door: These were the faces of this war. It was present tense. My brother joined the navy but never got beyond Guam. Boys I knew did see action. Some came home and some didn't. History in the making didn't feel like history.

While the war wound on and then down, I became a college teacher. These were years I spent well in an honorable vocation. Yet like my father I had missed the war of my generation, and the thirty years that separated my father and me were bridged by this fact. I began to understand what it meant for a man to live between wars.

The war finally ended. Its veterans, young men near my own age, found their way to the campus where I taught: Some as students, some as officers in the ROTC, many in support positions. They were my students or they were among the guys I played ball with in the noon league. Sometimes as teacher or academic advisor, sometimes as friend, I heard their war stories. A very few were obsessed, their minds scarred, but most shared as my old coach had or as I imagine my grandfather speaking.

Now twenty-five years later, veterans are still finishing up degrees, still my students. Some of them, like me, are the old-timers of the noon basketball league, grey and balding men with more memories than moves. In the shower and locker room I look away from the twisting battle scars that a few of them carry on bodies otherwise as undistinguished in middle age as my own. All of us are a bit beyond our prime as we head into the uncertain history of the next century.

But the war years of the Sixties and Seventies that were so confusing at the time now have the feel of history. I've read *Dispatches* and seen *Platoon*, and they are not like reading *Catch 22* or seeing *The Sands of Iwo Jima*. In my mind the Vietnam War cannot fade into the deeper past of my father's war. And because it can't, I think I know finally the conflicting emotions that my father felt for staying home, for missing a war, for not taking an ultimate risk, for being spared. I understand his deference to his contemporaries who fought and to their stories. I, too, feel a peculiar if misguided envy of my contemporaries who faced war directly. I suppose my regret is cousin to guilt. I ask, "What if?" What if I had gone? There is an anxiety in the unanswered questions, and that quiet cousin to guilt seeks absolution. But from whom?

In a given century most men don't go to war. The odds are always that some will be too old and others too young. Most of us will hear rather than tell war stories. I think of my soldier grandfather and of my father, myself, and my son. And given a choice, I wish that my son lives between wars. I would rather he hear than tell stories of war.

Epilogue

Amazing Grace and the Magic Cube

TWO YOUNG SKATEBOARDERS "ollied" the curbs in the Lloyd Center parking lot. In the joy of their play they seemed immune to both gravity and the heat of the summer day. Had I paused to watch, I suspect the play would have quickly become an exhibition. It would have been typical behavior. Many creatures play, but only in humanity has performance become so defining an attribute. I left them and sought out the cool shadows of the shopping mall. I made no pretense of shopping. This was simply a morning of window gazing and people watching. The smell of freshly made Karmel Corn and the first notes, barely audible, of some distant music floated among the real shoppers. The notes grew into a chorus of voices, and the promise of still another live performance drew me forward.

"How sweet the sound," they sang, and I moved across the mall expecting to find a raised platform with choir and instruments amidst a crowd. The rhythm of this "Amazing Grace" favored soft rock rather than gospel; still the reverberations off the walls and display windows were inspiring and spiritual. But I found neither singers nor musicians. And no crowd had gathered. There was a platform left over from some other event, but it was empty. "Tis grace has brought me safe thus far" rose from a recording played over the loudspeaker in the skating rink below the main level of the mall.

On the white rink a pair of figure skaters had the ice to themselves. No spangles, no electric colors. This was a practice session. The couple was not young, but this showed only in the lines of their faces not in the lines they cut on the ice. They spun and twirled, at times joined only by his hand gripping hers against the centrifugal force of their rotations. Their skates etched complicated patterns, and against the white surface of the rink their bodies moved like animated musical notations across an unscored piece of paper.

They attracted a crowd. Though they hadn't intended it, practice became performance. We watched them and marveled at their grace. Our heads moved in small circles as our eyes tried to join in their dance around the rink. We were no longer shoppers, people watchers, or coffee breakers; we had become an audience. We followed them as musicians follow a conductor.

The skaters never looked up. But as the crowd became an audience, they moved with a new energy and intensity. The silent appreciation that we showered on them carried also an expectation. They had to move *for* us as well as *with* the music. Our expectation had a sharpness as keen as the steel blades that touched the ice. We touched them too; an audience does that: Touches and holds a performer even as it is held and touched. And it is a precarious and tenuous hold, as balanced as a thin blade on ice.

"We've no less days to sing God's praise than when we'd first begun." The recording ended. Applause. And for the first time the skaters looked up and acknowledged their audience with a bow. We became shoppers again though we had just purchased something by our participation as an audience. And I've thought about that purchase, that exchange of good, between most audiences and performers. It is perhaps one of the basic currencies of our culture. It involves something learned and something nurtured as well as something spontaneous and something instinctive.

For a year I've watched this exchange and have been fascinated as much by audiences as performers. I suppose the source of amazement for me is how in a culture that seems so dedicated to the individual and so reliant on mass media we have nonetheless filled our lives with communal, almost tribal, events. Perhaps we call them community gatherings; a church or school hall decorated with paper streamers will do. It could be a grammar-school talent show where nervous mothers who have volunteered as stage managers lean from behind curtains to nudge a parade of performers into the light of the stage. And in the darkness the other members of the family sit waiting to enjoy and approve. Yet there is a benign tension, a masked seriousness, that bestows an importance on such an evening. One sees it in the restraint that is imposed on the youngest members of the audience. In the ways, not always successful, used to show them how to sit still, how to become a watcher, a listener, a part of an audience.

The first performer in the talent show, a Korean girl in traditional dress, sings a Korean folk song. She is followed by her brother who puffs his way through a martial art *hyung* in his Tae Kwon Do uniform and yellow belt. He makes a mistake, shakes his head, and puffs through the *hyung* again. Finished, he bows curtly as he seeks anonymity behind the curtain. A poised fifth grader in a high colored and ruffled dress renders a very slow sampling of Chopin on a piano that has just been rolled onto the stage by several of the larger boys. Her exit is demure and proper. One tiny fellow with huge owlish eyes, a boy who draws whispers of "how cute" from the audience, attempts a solo performance of "La Bamba" accompanied by the tallest of the fifth graders who backs him up on an electric guitar. The little fellow forgets the words halfway through. The older boy manages to whisper them and delay his fingering to rescue the number. The microphones pick up his whisper and every once in a while whine unaccountably on their own. These, too, become part of the program.

The stagehands place a small table in the center of the stage. From behind the curtain walks a boy in a rumpled plastic cape and top hat. He is very serious and carries a brown paper bag. He seems oblivious of the audience. Like an aged shopper home from the grocery store, he empties his bag of tricks. He stoops to the bag and lifts his paraphernalia to the table with the deliberateness of an old man. He performs each of his tricks with the same kind of deliberateness, but his powers fail him. The disappearing ball doesn't disappear. The rope cut in half doesn't magically come out of a bottle in one piece: Both pieces fall and stay in the bottle. His most spectacular trick needs an assistant, and a smaller version of himself, undoubtedly a younger brother, assists him with the magic cube trick. Each side of the cube has a different color. The assistant selects one side, shows it to the audience but not the magician, and then places the cube in a special box. The magician will now remove the cube from the box that he holds behind his back. Without looking at box or cube he will tell us the color. But each time he takes the cube from the box, his sympathetic assistant whispers: "It's the red one. It's the blue one." Caught between his unfortunate apprentice and his desire to accomplish the trick, the little sorcerer can only begin over and over.

He is released from his dilemma only when the laughter from the audience drowns out the whispers from the too-helpful assistant. When he bows, his plastic hat falls off and the audience roars. He puts the hat back on his head and in his nervous confusion bows once more. The hat falls off again, and the audience claps all the harder. A failed magician has become an exquisite entertainer. This is a different kind of magic: Creating laughter and applause from silence. The boy lets his face find its natural smile and finally takes his leave.

We applauded his willingness to remain on stage, to endure the lights and our eyes, to stand alone. And our laughter is an affectionate appreciation of the humanity that he embodies. Unwittingly he and his misguided apprentice have acted out the comedy of the human situation. For a few moments their unscripted comic routine mirrored Beckett's *Waiting for Godot.* They were a pint-sized Estragon and Vladimir. And their performance had drawn our sympathy and laughter.

The magician played before a home crowd, an extension of his family. It is the way that most of us begin. It is an initiation and a rite of passage. Sometimes it is harder to appear before those who are closest to us even if we can presume their affection and understanding. All subsequent performances are touched with the awe of that first nervous venture. To step from the crowd, to perform, is to take on a responsibility and a risk. And to watch is to become potential judge as well as audience. I believe that only a cynical and jaded professional could ever escape from the nearly primordial tension that fuels any performance.

As a youngster I never had the talent to take center stage. My own experiences of the tension and excitement of performing were always qualified by my position in the last rows of a choir or chorus—the unhappy but safe fate of those of us born with tin ears and two left feet. But last spring I was invited to appear with the University Choir and Singers in a presentation of "Frostiana," a choral arrangement of seven Robert Frost poems. Though I was not trusted with a singing part, I would stand in front of the choir, quite alone, read from Frost, and present a commentary. It was as close as I would ever come to being a performer.

My audience was sympathetic and interested, and before I rose from my chair to address them, I noted many familiar and friendly faces. But as I began "Whose woods these are I think I know," I was no longer conscious of particular faces. Carried by Frost's pentameter, I felt as if I too had happened upon some lonely wood, that I stood in the clearing of some psychological forest. But that impression was not accurate. I was not alone and I was in the light. And what music there was in my voice carried to the audience; and their attention, which felt palpable as I recited, drew me out. Together we repeated a common occurrence of our species. Of an evening we had come together to let one of us speak or sing or dance in the shared light while the great darkness of night took possession beyond our gathering. To my gathering I read on, "But I have promises to keep, and miles to go before I sleep." So do we all, and the performances in our lives are one of the pauses, one of the graces, that ease the shared journey.

Acknowledgments

ALONG THE WAY TO becoming a book, these essays have passed through the hands of skilled and generous editors. I wish to acknowledge my debt to John Soisson and Brian Doyle, editors of *Portland*, and Keith Petersen of Washington State University Press. My thanks also to Christy Schuck and Sharon Rossmiller for help in preparing the manuscript, Jo Savage for the book design, and Beth DeWeese for the marketing expertise. And to Father John Chaplin, Father Terry Lally, and Padre Arthur Schoenfeldt a special thanks for seeing the writer through a hard passage. Without the support and sacrifices of my family, this book never would have been written.